Designed to make Florida gardening easier.

Volume 3 - *Stormscaping*

During the hurricanes of 2004 and 2005, how much property damage was done by wind-sensitive vegetation that could have been avoided? Pamela Crawford has researched and analyzed thousands of pages of data and spoken to hundreds of experts - such as Max Mayfield, the director of the National Hurricane Center, 37 different county extension agents, and researchers from University of Florida - and found answers that every Floridian needs to know. What are the best and worst trees for wind? How can you position strong trees to actually protect your home? *Stormscaping* will teach you this and much more to help you minimize damage during the next big one!

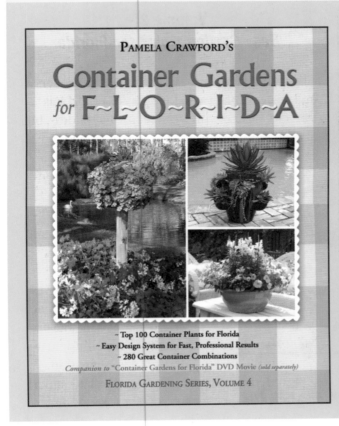

Volume 4 - *Container Gardens for Florida*

From the author: "I spent the last few years testing over 7000 plants and hundreds of containers to learn which ones give the best performance with the least amount of care in my Florida garden. I have especially looked for methods of using containers for maximum design impact, like the huge hanging baskets I've seen in England. After my usual number of early failures, I have had some great successes, and am very excited about this book." It not only covers the best plants and containers but also great methods of designing with these containers in your garden. This book, with 350 pages, will be an excellent source of ideas as well as a major reference book for years to come.

© 2001, 2002, 2003, 2004, 2005, 2007 Color Garden Inc.

First Printing, 2001
Second Printing, 2002
Third Printing, 2002
Fourth Printing, 2003
Fifth Printing, 2004
Sixth Printing, 2005
Seventh Printing, 2007

Library of Congress Catalog Card Number pending

ISBN number: 0-9712220-0-2

Printed in Korea by Asianprinting.com

This book is available at most book stores, many garden centers, and from most internet book sellers. To locate your nearest source or to order wholesale, contact:

Color Garden Publishing
1353 Riverstone Parkway, Suite 120-372, Canton, GA 30114
Phone: 561-964-6500 Fax: 561-967-6205 Email: colorgdn@aol.com
Website: www.easygardencolor.com

To locate plants, go to www.easygardencolor.com.

Photos by Pamela Crawford except for:

Gene Joiner: Ilex on page 28. Juniper on page 32. Firebush on page 84. Podocarpus on pages 106, 177, 249, 251, 261, 262, 269, 270, 271. Petrea on pages 128, 129, 250. White Bird close-up on page 151. Geiger Tree and close-up of the flower on pages 68, 76, 156, 157, 271, 272, 303. Cattley Guava leaves and fruit on page 161. Both Royal Poinciana photos on page 173 and 262. Laurel Oak on pages 178,245,251,255,265,270,272. Palmettos on page 217,249,250,262. Cast Iron Plant on page 242. Snake Plant on page 242.

All before and after landscape design: Pamela Crawford, Color Garden Inc., Lake Worth, Florida

Installation: Tom Homrich Landscaping, Heritage Farms Nursery, Lake Worth, Florida of all the gardens except: Plant installations on pages 238, 239, 241, 266, 278, 279, and accessory installations on pages 273-275, which were done by Cindy Lou Corum of Color Garden Group, Loxatchee, Florida.

CONTENTS

EASY PLANTS

EASY GARDENS

ACKNOWLEDGEMENTS

One thing I love about the plant business is the people. Whenever I had a question about anything, people always gave me their time and attention. I would like to especially thank the following:

Special thanks to Gene Joyner, Palm Beach County Extension Service in West Palm Beach, Florida, for the many hours and weeks spent checking all the horticultural data.

Bruce Adams, South Florida Water Management District, West Palm Beach, Florida: information on the water situation.

Dr. Frank Brown, Valkaria, Florida: information on Crotons and Ti Plants

John Coatti, Wellington, Florida: proofreading

Cindy Lou Corum, Color Garden Group (Lake Worth and Loxahatchee, Florida): plant installations on pages 238, 239, 241, 266, 278, 279. Accessory installations on pages 273 -275.

John Doyle, Loving Care Landscape, Lake Worth, Florida: horticultural and computer help, especially the information on trimming.

Dorris Happel, Boynton Beach, Florida: proofreading

Tom Homrich, Tom Homrich Landscaping and Heritage Farms Nursery, Lake Worth, Florida: tree information and installation of most of the gardens in this book.

Robin Jamieson, Paradise Landscaping, Boynton Beach, Florida: horticultural information.

Joe Lawson, Palm Beach County School Board, West Palm Beach, Florida: horticultural information.

Katherine Maidman, Curator of Palms, Fairchild Tropical Gardens, Miami, Florida: information on palms.

David McLean, Ft. Lauderdale, Florida: horticultural information

Craig Morrell, Horticulturist at Boca Raton Resort and Club, Boca Raton, Florida: horticultural information.

Elise Ryan, Color Garden Farms Nursery, Loxahatchee, Florida: grower of most of the plant material.

WHAT ARE EASY PLANTS?

One of my trial gardens

Criteria for inclusion of plants in this book:

1. Ability to withstand summer rains and heat

2. General resistance to pests in the landscape after an initial establishment period

3. Attractive appearance with trimming three times a year or less

4. Need water twice a week or less after initial establishment period

5. Consistent behavior for at least two years in multiple locations

6. Ability to adapt to a variety of urban and suburban situations

7. Plants of various heights and environmental tolerances to provide a complete plant palette for many residences and commercial establishments.

8. Ability to coexist on the same irrigation zones as St. Augustine grass

9. Tolerance to native soils

INTRODUCTION

WHAT ARE EASY PLANTS?

Above: One of my trial gardens

For the last 10 years, I have been testing plants in Palm Beach County, looking for the ones that give the most impact for the least amount of care. Out of approximately 2500 I have tested, only 200 have passed my trials. Most of them die during the first summer, not having the ability to withstand either our heat or our summer rains. I probably hold the record for killing plants in south Florida.

I am quite excited about the plants that have passed my trials. Easy gardens have provided wonderful experiences for me because, for years, I did not think that they were possible in south Florida.

For this book, I chose 100 easy plants that are very well adapted to the south Florida environment. They are generally adaptable, taking the routine extremes our climate offers. Although I found more than 100 easy plants in my trials, I focused on plants that have widespread landscape potential. I also included a complete plant palette, so that someone could complete a residence or commercial building using only the plants in this book.

Trimming requires the most labor of any maintenance chore in south Florida. The easy plants in this book require trimming no more than three times a year. This criteria shut out a lot of my favorite plants, like Bougainvillea, but I felt it was very important to identify plants that do not require much time to maintain.

My extensive experience in landscape design has exposed me to many different tastes in plants. The ones in this book are plants that most people like.

Trial gardens as viewed from my desk, where I wrote this book. Each plant is tested for at least two years in my gardens prior to more extensive testing in many different types of environments.

Before

After

INTRODUCTION

GOALS OF THIS BOOK

<u>Enhance the south Florida environment for all its residents:</u> The more variety I plant, the more wild creatures I see enjoying the garden with me. Wildlife are like people - you would not want the same meal every night. They like variety. All the animal photos throughout this book were photographed in my gardens.

I have shared my gardens with the gentleness of Hummingbirds and the fierceness of nesting Alligators, the shyness of the Great Blue Heron and the quietness of the Coral Snake. None of these creatures has ever hurt me. Sometimes there are so many butterflies, they look like clouds of flying flowers.

Diversification of commonly used plants, coupled with saving as much of our natural environment as we can fight for, will do a lot to save our remaining wild creatures.

<u>Educate:</u> I hope this book can dispel the common myths that flowering plants require more care than green plants, that plants need a lot of water to look good, and that summer is a bad time to plant. I hope gardeners will understand the size the plant needs to be to thrive and use it accordingly and understand that shade is a great place for garden color.

<u>Beautify:</u> I hope this book gives people ideas for beautifying their homes. The potential for beautifying the south Florida environment, both public and private, is staggering.

<u>Enjoy:</u> I hope this book brings joy to gardeners throughout south Florida. I walk through my gardens daily, marveling at the flowers that nature created and the creatures that enjoy them with me.

I attempted to make as much information as possible self-explanatory on the plant pages. Some additional explanations are necessary:

<u>Growth Rate:</u> The growth rate greatly depends on the plants' environment. More water and fertilizer, for example, cause plants to grow faster, so the categories are estimates only. *Slow* refers to a plant that increases its size by less than 20 percent the first year. *Medium* refers to a plant that increases its size by 20 to 50 per cent the first year. *Fast* refers to plants that grow more than 50 per cent during the first year in the ground.

<u>On Center:</u> Measurement from the center of one plant to the center of another

<u>Salt Tolerance:</u> *Low* refers to plants that do not tolerate salt spray on their leaves. *Medium* refers to plants that take some salt on their leaves. *High* refers to plants that take direct oceanfront conditions, provided they are somewhat back from the shoreline. The chapter titled "Easy Salt and Wind Gardens" (page 266) gives more detail.

<u>Wind Tolerance:</u> *Low* refers to plants that like fairly protected locations. *Medium* refers to plants that take medium wind. *High* refers to plants that are the most wind tolerant we have. In storms where winds reach 30 to 40 miles per hour for more than a few hours, even plants with high wind tolerance suffer leaf burn. However, the plants with high wind tolerance sustain less damage than the ones with low wind tolerance. The leaf burn does not heal. New leaves grow and eventually replace the ones that are damaged. None of the plants in this book can sustain severe tropical storm or hurricane force winds without damage.

<u>Zone:</u> The USDA has developed plant hardiness zones that refer to the temperature ranges the plants tolerate. **<u>This book is written for south Florida, defined as zones 10a, 10b, and 11.</u>**

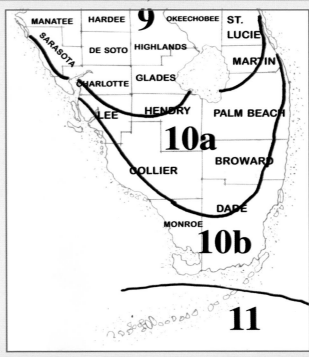

Average minimum temperatures:
  Zone 10a: 30 to 35 degrees
  Zone 10b: 35 to 40 degrees
  Zone 11: Over 40 degrees

DEDICATION

This book is dedicated to my husband, George Kirkham, who believed in me and made this book possible...

...and to my son, Ryan Crawford, who enthusiastically embraced my crazy plan to leave our comfortable house and move into a cabin in the woods...

...and to all the creatures who share our little woods with us.

CHAPTER 1

GROUNDCOVERS AND SMALL SHRUBS
6 TO 24 INCHES TALL

Left and above: Ground Orchids (Spathoglottis plicata)

Botanical Name: *Acalypha pendula*

Common Name: **Dwarf or Trailing Chenille**

CHARACTERISTICS

PLANT TYPE: Groundcover

AVERAGE SIZE: About 6 inches tall by 12 to 18 inches wide.

GROWTH RATE: Medium

LEAF: Medium to light green; about 1 inch long.

FLOWER: Dark red, long, and furry like a caterpillar. Size varies from about 2 inches long by 1/2 inch wide to 3 inches long by about 3/4 inch wide.

BEST COLOR: Most of the year.

AVERAGE LIFE: Unknown exactly, but trials so far show at least 2 years on the average.

ORIGIN: Unknown

CAUTIONS: None known

SPACING: 12 to 18 inches on center.

One of the few groundcovers for south Florida that grows flat to the ground and flowers most of the time.

Dwarf Chenille is the groundcover in front. Sanchezia is the variegated plant in back. Bromeliads inhabit the trees.

General: Dwarf Chenille is a new plant in south Florida. I have only been using it for about two years, so I still have a lot to learn about it. It has traditionally been used primarily in hanging baskets and is a great container plant. I have found it quite useful in the landscape because it is among the few subtropical plants that stays so low. Most of the plant species that stay this low have died after a few months in my trials. This one has lasted two years so far and blooms happily in sun or shade.

Companions: Dwarf Chenille is a very versatile plant, blending with any landscape style. Since it grows well in sun or shade, it works as a border for most of the plants in this book. To show it best, mix with other colors that contrast with the red.

Dwarf Chenille and some companions

GROWING CONDITIONS

LIGHT: Medium shade to full sun. Untested in deep shade.

WATER: After initial establishment period, medium. Ideal is once a week in shade, twice a week in sun or wind. Tolerates irrigation up to 3 times a week. Untested without irrigation.

SOIL: Wide range, as long as it is well drained.

SALT TOLERANCE: Untested. Other types of Acalyphas have a medium salt tolerance.

WIND TOLERANCE: Untested.

ZONE: 10a to 11

PEST PROBLEMS: None known.

PROPAGATION: Cuttings

Care in the Landscape: Dwarf Chenille is relatively easy to grow. However, it has a tendency to try to escape its area and run up other plants. Maintain some space around the Chenille for trimming, as shown opposite, so that it cannot get into the nearby plants. Dwarf Chenille needs regular fertilization. Apply a well-balanced, slow-release mix that contains minor elements in March, June, and October. If the leaves yellow in-between regular fertilizations, fertilize again.

Botanical Name: *Aechmea 'Mend' cv. of lueddemanniana*

Common Name: **Mend Bromeliad**

CHARACTERISTICS

PLANT TYPE: Groundcover

AVERAGE SIZE: 12 to 24 inches tall with a 24 to 36 inch spread at maturity.

GROWTH RATE: Slow

LEAF: Pink and green striped; about 8 inches long.

FLOWER: Long spike that appears once a year in spring with berries on the end. Not as glamorous as many Bromeliad flowers. Use this plant for leaf color.

BEST COLOR: No seasonal variation.

AVERAGE LIFE: Single plant lives about 2 years but sends up babies to replace itself. A clump of good landscape bromeliads lasts indefinitely.

ORIGIN: Tropical America

CAUTIONS: Leaves have spines. Wear long sleeves when handling.

SPACING: 2 feet on center

A tough landscape bromeliad that gives constant color with very little care. Takes more light than most bromeliads.

Mend Bromeliads do well in pots, hung in trees, or planted in the ground.

General: Many beautiful bromeliads have appeared on the market in the last few years. I have not tested all of them but have tested enough to know that many do not do well in the south Florida landscape. The biggest problem is the failure of the glamorous flower to reappear after its initial bloom. There are many that do flower again. To be sure, ask the nursery what their experiences have been in the landscape with the bromeliad you consider buying. The Mend Bromeliad gives year-round color from its leaves and has proved its hardiness hundreds of times. This Bromeliad takes more sun than most and lives happily in the shade as well.

Companions: The Mend Bromeliad combines beautifully with plants that have flowers or leaves in the same shade of pink. Try it with Angelwing Begonias, Caricature Plants, and Starburst Pentas. It is also a great companion for ferns.

Mend Bromeliads with Starburst Pentas and Blue Daze

GROWING CONDITIONS

LIGHT: Medium to light shade; the pink color fades in deep shade or full sun. This bromeliad takes more sun than most but burns with too many hours of sun a day, particularly midday sun.

WATER: After initial establishment period, low. Ideal is once every week or two. Bromeliads rot with too much water. Tolerates irrigation up to 2 or 3 times a week but needs much less. Untested without irrigation.

SOIL: Wide range, if well drained.

SALT TOLERANCE: Medium

WIND TOLERANCE: High

ZONE: 10a to 11

PEST PROBLEMS: Fungus with too much water.

PROPAGATION: Offshoots

Care in the Landscape: The mother plant dies after flowering and producing pups (babies). Trim off the dead plant after it becomes brown. Leave the remaining pups to grow where they are or separate them to cover more ground. Since this only has to be done every year or two, this is truly an easy plant. No fertilization is required unless faster growth is desired. Do not put fertilizer in the center well of the plant.

Botanical Name: *Asparagus densiflorus 'Myers'*

Common Name: **Foxtail Fern**

CHARACTERISTICS

PLANT TYPE: Groundcover

AVERAGE SIZE: Easily maintained at sizes between 12 inches tall by 8 inches wide and 24 inches tall by 18 inches wide.

GROWTH RATE: Medium

LEAF: Lime green; plume-like, about 12 to 24 inches long.

FLOWER: Inconspicuous

BEST COLOR: No seasonal variation.

AVERAGE LIFE: 2 to 10 years.

ORIGIN: South Africa

CAUTIONS: Expect to lose about 5% of these plants during the first few months in the ground. They do not die completely, but grow poorly and slowly. Replace as necessary.

SPACING: 12 to 18 inches on center.

A unique groundcover that gives an interesting texture to the garden with very little care.

Foxtail Fern in the landscape

General: The Foxtail Fern is an excellent source of texture in the garden. If all plants have the same texture in an area, they run together visually. The eye is unable to separate the masses. The shape of the Foxtail Fern is unique and excellent for breaking up masses.

Ti Red Sister   *Variegated Arboricola*   *Mammey Croton*

Some companions

Companions: Use Foxtail Ferns with other green textures. Bright colors that look good with Foxtails include Ti Plants and Crotons. Foxtails are also interesting borders for flower gardens and good companions for rocks and Bromeliads.

Below: Palms, Xanadus, and Junipers combine with Foxtail Ferns for a green, textured look.

Before

After

GROWING CONDITIONS

LIGHT: Medium shade to full sun.

WATER: After initial establishment period, low water. Ideal is once a week. Tolerates irrigation up to 3 times a week. Survives without irrigation in average environmental conditions.

SOIL: Wide range

SALT TOLERANCE: Medium

WIND TOLERANCE: Medium (untested in high wind).

ZONE: 10a to 11

PEST PROBLEMS: None known.

PROPAGATION: Seeds, division.

Care in the Landscape: Foxtail Ferns are easy to grow but somewhat sporadic (see 'CAUTIONS', opposite). Fertilize in March, June, and October with a well-balanced, slow-release mix with minor elements. Trim to remove brown leaves and to even out the height of the clumps. Divide clumps about every five years.

Botanical Name: *Codiaeum variegatum 'Mammey'*

Common Name: **Mammey Croton or Fire Croton**

CHARACTERISTICS

PLANT TYPE: Shrub or groundcover.

AVERAGE SIZE: Easily maintained at sizes between 1 foot tall by 1 foot wide and 5 feet tall by 4 feet wide.

GROWTH RATE: Slow; takes many years to reach full height of 5 feet. Almost no growth in winter.

LEAF: Brightly colored in shades of red, yellow, and green; about 1 inch wide and 6 to 8 inches long; slightly wider than Corkscrew Croton leaves, but with the same twisted form.

FLOWER: Insignificant

BEST COLOR: All year

AVERAGE LIFE: 15 to 20 years.

ORIGIN: Malaysia. Mammey is a hybrid.

CAUTIONS: Milky sap is an irritant and can stain clothes. (I work with Crotons frequently and have never stained my clothing.)

SPACING: 12 to 18 inches on center.

One of the most colorful groundcovers available. The only Croton I found that can be maintained as short as 12 inches. Constant color with very little care.

Close-up of Fire Croton or Mammey Croton. The leaves reflect the bright colors of fire.

General: Most groundcovers that can be maintained as low as twelve inches have a very short life-span or require a lot of care. The Mammey Croton is among the few that lives for 15 to 20 years with very little maintenance. These characteristics, coupled with the fact that it displays its strong colors all year, make it one of the most useful plants for the low maintenance garden. This plant is more aptly called the Fire Croton than Mammey Croton because its leaves reflect the bright colors of fire. Because of its vibrant tones, this Croton can set the color scheme for an entire garden.

Companions: Mammey Crotons work particularly well with plants that have leaves or flowers that are red or yellow. An easy garden with dramatic color could feature Firespikes in the center, Shrimps next, and Mammey Crotons as a border. Another easy combination features Yellow Mussaendas in the center and Fire Crotons next with a border of Dwarf Chenille.

Mammey Crotons form a border for Ti Red Sisters and Shrimp plants.

Care in the Landscape: Mammey Crotons are very easy to grow. They appreciate fertilizing in March, June, and October with a well-balanced, slow-release mix that contains minor elements. To encourage fullness, pinch off the tips of the branches about once a year. If the plant gets leggy, cut stalks way back (to two inches) in summer. Trim as needed to maintain desired size and to keep masses at equal heights. Mammey Crotons are generally sold with three plants in each pot. These multiples allow you to stagger the cuts on the stems at different heights to keep the height of the plant and avoid legginess.

Botanical Name: *Euphorbia milii 'Rosy'*

Common Name: **Dwarf Crown of Thorns, Rosy Crown of Thorns**

CHARACTERISTICS

PLANT TYPE: Shrub or groundcover.

AVERAGE SIZE: Easily maintained at sizes between 18 inches tall by 14 inches wide and 3 feet tall by 2 feet wide.

GROWTH RATE: Slow

LEAF: Medium green; about 1 inch long.

FLOWER: Bright pink, almost red clusters of flowers; each flower is about 1/2 inch wide.

BEST COLOR: One of the few plants that blooms constantly except when the temperature dips to the 40's.

AVERAGE LIFE: 10 to 15 years, if not overwatered.

ORIGIN: Madagascar

CAUTIONS: Wear gloves when handling; the milky sap is toxic and may cause a rash.

SPACING: 24 inches on center. Although plants may seem too far apart when young, they will not grow well if placed closer.

One of the few flowering plants that can be kept pruned below two feet and still produces blooms.

Rosy Crown of Thorns viewed from above

GENERAL: One of the biggest requests of the plant industry is for a plant that stays small, blooms constantly, lasts ten years, and requires little care. The only plant I know that meets this criteria is the Rosy Crown of Thorns, one of the newer Crown of Thorn cultivars. People like the Crown of Thorns for its color and compact shape, not for its legginess and thorns. The Rosy Crown of Thorns is much easier to keep neat and compact than most of the older varieties. The compact growth habit is ideal - naturally developing into a round, compact ball. The thorns, which are much softer than the older varieties, are difficult to see. Requiring trimming only once every year or two, the Rosy Crown of Thorns is one of the easiest sources of color in the subtropical plant world. It is also among the few colorful plants that thrives in salt and wind environments.

Companions: Use the Rosy Crown of Thorns as a groundcover for any size area or as a border in front of taller shrubs. It fits well in a manicured garden. One of the most colorful, low maintenance plant palettes includes Variegated Arboricola Trinettes as the back layer, Mammey Crotons in the middle, and Rosy Crown of Thorns as a border. This Crown of Thorns is also an excellent border for Philodendron Xanadu.

Rosy Crown of Thorns bordering Fire Crotons and Sanchezias

Care in the Landscape: During the first year or two of planting, trim infrequently to maintain shape. As soon as the shrub grows out of its neat, compact shape, prune heavily, back to sticks. Restrict heavy pruning to summer months. Trim to restore the round shape, not to square it off. The Rosy Crown of Thorns is not a heavy feeder. It benefits and grows faster from fertilization in March, June, and October with a well-balanced, slow-release mix that contains minor elements.

Note: Many new dwarf Crown of Thorn cultivars are appearing on the market. I tested five or six others besides Rosy. They all died from fungus. I'm sure more good ones will eventually be developed, but be careful.

GROWING CONDITIONS

LIGHT: Full sun. Some other types of Crown of Thorns take some shade, but not this one.

WATER: After initial establishment period, low water. Ideal is once a week. Tolerates irrigation up to twice a week. Overwatering causes fungus, the most common problem with this plant. Survives without irrigation in average environmental conditions.

SOIL: Wide range, if well drained.

SALT TOLERANCE: High

WIND TOLERANCE: High

ZONE: 10b to 11. Leaves darken in response to cold.

PEST PROBLEMS: Fungus is a problem during rainy years. Watch for black spots and yellow leaves. If possible, cut back on watering. If fungus becomes severe, treat with a fungicide. The Rosy Crown of Thorns has fewer problems with fungus than any other dwarf variety I tested.

PROPAGATION: Cuttings; Let the cuttings dry for a day or 2 before planting. Do not keep leaves or soil constantly moist when rooting. Water only when the soil is very dry.

Botanical Name: *Evolvulus glomeratus*

Common Name: **Blue Daze**

CHARACTERISTICS

PLANT TYPE: Groundcover

AVERAGE SIZE: 12 inches tall by 12 to 18 inches wide.

GROWTH RATE: Medium

LEAF: Grayish green; about 3/4 inch long.

FLOWER: Blue; about 3/4 inch wide.

BEST COLOR: Most of the year, but flowers close in extreme heat. Blue Daze blooms best in winter.

AVERAGE LIFE: 1 to 3 years. Short-lived but inexpensive, easy, and useful.

ORIGIN: South America

CAUTIONS: None known

SPACING: 12 to 24 inches on center.

Low growing, cool weather bloomer with a unique blue flower. Short-lived but tolerant of salt, sun, wind, or shade.

Close-up of Blue Daze

General: Although short-lived, Blue Daze is a valuable asset to the subtropical garden. Very few perennials stay this low, bloom in sun or shade, and tolerate salt environments. The blue color is unique, although it does not show up well alone or with other green plants. Mix it with other colors, especially yellow and pink, to show it off best. Blue Daze is an inexpensive alternative to annuals.

Pink Ruellia Katie　　*Yellow Mussaenda*

Some companions

Companions: Blue Daze looks best mixed with other colors. It is a great border for yellow or pink flowering shrubs, like the Shrimp, Yellow Mussaenda, Walking Iris, Pentas, and Angelwing Begonia. It is also attractive as a groundcover under small flowering trees, like the Golden Senna, Cassia Tree, and Anderson Crepe Hibiscus.

Blue Daze with Cranberry Pentas and Yellow Lantanas

LIGHT: Medium shade to full sun. Not dense shade.

WATER: After initial establishment period, medium water. Needs more than average water while becoming established in the landscape. After establishment, overwatering is the biggest enemy of Blue Daze. Ideal water is once a week in shade or twice a week in sun or wind. Untested without irrigation.

SOIL: Wide range, if well-drained.

SALT TOLERANCE: High; an excellent source of color in a high salt environment.

WIND TOLERANCE: High

ZONE: 10b to 11

PEST PROBLEMS: Fungus and scale. To minimize problems, do not overwater or plant too deeply.

PROPAGATION: Cuttings

Care in the Landscape: Blue Daze is quite easy to grow. Trim occasionally to maintain desired size. Blue Daze benefits from a hard cutback in the summer so that air can circulate during the wettest months. The biggest enemy of Blue Daze is fungus, and air circulation diminishes its onset. Fertilize in March, June, and October with a well-balanced, slow-release mix that contains minor elements.

Botanical Name: *Hymenocallis latifolia*

Common Name: **Spider Lily**

CHARACTERISTICS

PLANT TYPE: Groundcover

AVERAGE SIZE: 2 to 3 feet tall, growing in spreading clusters.

GROWTH RATE: Medium

LEAF: Medium green; shaped like a long, thick blade of grass. About 1/2 inch wide by 2 feet long.

FLOWER: White, beautiful, about 5 inches long by 4 inches wide.

BEST COLOR: Spring to early summer. Short bloom period.

AVERAGE LIFE: At least 10 years.

ORIGIN: Florida

CAUTIONS: Poisonous

SPACING: 12 inches on center.

Used primarily for its foliage, this native occasionally blooms with a spectacular flower.

Close-up of the flower. The bloom period is quite short.

General: The Spider Lily is native groundcover used primarily for its attractive leaves. Although the flower is spectacular, use the Spider Lily for its foliage because the bloom period is very short. It is quite useful as a groundcover, massed in areas where texture is important to the overall design.

Companions: Use Spider Lilies with other textures. They work well to break up masses of Dwarf Fakahatchee Grass and Liriope. Fishtail Ferns and Wart Ferns are also attractive with Spider Lilies. For contrast, border masses of Spider Lilies with Purple Queen and Dwarf Chenille. Spider Lilies are also attractive planted in a mass under Thatch Palms.

Although the flower (opposite page) is spectacular, use the Spider Lily primarily for its foliage, which is what you see for most of the year.

Care in the Landscape: Spider Lilies are very easy to grow. We have not touched the ones in our trial gardens since they were planted over five years ago. They have a few leaf spots but look very good overall. For faster growth, fertilize in March, June, and October with a well-balanced, slow-release mix with minor elements.

GROWING CONDITIONS

LIGHT: Light shade to full sun.

WATER: After initial establishment, low water. Ideal is once a week. Tolerates very wet situations as well. Survives without irrigation in average environmental conditions.

SOIL: Wide range

SALT TOLERANCE: High

WIND TOLERANCE: Unknown

ZONE: 10a to 11

PEST PROBLEMS: Lubber grasshoppers.

PROPAGATION: Seeds, division, bulbs. Slow to propagate by seed. Faster by bulbs.

Botanical Name: *Ilex vomitoria 'Stokes Dwarf'*

Common Name: **Dwarf Ilex or Ilex Stokes**

CHARACTERISTICS

PLANT TYPE: Groundcover or small shrub.

AVERAGE SIZE: Easily maintained at sizes between 12 inches tall by 12 inches wide and 6 feet tall by 4 feet wide.

GROWTH RATE: Slow

LEAF: Tiny, 1/8 inch; gray-green with a slight iridescence.

FLOWER: Inconspicuous

BEST COLOR: No seasonal variation.

AVERAGE LIFE: Unknown, but decades.

ORIGIN: Southeast U.S.

CAUTIONS: As the name suggests (vomitoria), eating this plant makes you sick.

SPACING: 10 to 12 inches on center for a low hedge.

The best hedge material for low, neat hedges. Slow growing and easy to maintain.

Ilex about six months after planting. This plant requires patience to form a hedge because it is very slow growing.

General: Dwarf Ilex is useful primarily for low, neatly trimmed hedges. It is a very dense plant that shears beautifully. Small hedges are useful, not only in formal gardens, but also to separate different sections in geometric gardens. These geometric or partitioned gardens are commonly used in England and Italy. This plant is quite cold tolerant and easy to care for with little trimming, even in the most formal landscapes.

Cocoplum

Dwarf Ixora

Some companions for a manicured look

Companions: For layered hedges, use Lakeview Jasmine or Viburnum as the tallest layer, Silver Buttonwood as the middle layer, and border with Dwarf Ilex. The lighter color of the Buttonwood breaks up the dark green of the other layers. For herb or partitioned flower gardens, lay out a geometric pattern with the Ilex. Fill the sections with herbs or any of the flowering shrubs or groundcovers in this book. Be sure to keep the flowering plants some distance away from the Ilex. The small hedge needs light, and planting too close usually results in the faster growing, flowering material crushing the little hedge. For a low maintenance, manicured look with color, use Cocoplums as the back layer, Dwarf Ixoras in the middle, and border with Ilex.

Dwarf Ilex bordering flowers. The annual Salvias in the bed are on the verge of blooming.

Care in the Landscape: Ilex is not demanding of fertilizer. However, if faster growth is desired, fertilize in March, June, and October with a well-balanced, slow-release mix with minor elements. Shear as needed into a small hedge or rounded specimen.

Botanical Name: *Ixora 'Petite'*

Common Name: **Red Taiwan Dwarf Ixora**

CHARACTERISTICS

PLANT TYPE: Shrub

AVERAGE SIZE: Easily maintained at sizes between 18 inches tall by 12 inches wide and 4 feet tall by 3 feet wide. Included in the category of under 2 feet because that is its most common size in the landscape.

GROWTH RATE: Slow

LEAF: Medium green; about 2 inches long by 1/2 inch wide.

FLOWER: Orange-red cluster, about 2 to 3 inches wide.

BEST COLOR: Blooms all year in unusually warm years. In average years, stops blooming from January until March.

AVERAGE LIFE: 10 to 20 years.

ORIGIN: Most Ixoras are native to southern Asia. This one is a hybrid.

CAUTIONS: None known

SPACING: 18 to 24 inches on center.

One of the few plants that produces blooms for most of the year even when trimmed close. Can be maintained at shorter sizes than most shrubs.

Dwarf Ixora as a small hedge

General: The Dwarf Ixora is one of the few subtropical shrubs that can be kept short and still bloom. This miniature Ixora provides a lot of color with minimal care. Enjoying this plant requires patience. It grows very slowly and needs to fill out for a year or two after planting before it flowers significantly. Dwarf Ixora also comes in pink and yellow. The pink is lovely, but it has a much shorter bloom period and grows slower. I have not tested the yellow.

Variegated Arboricola   Mammey Croton   Juniper

Some companions

Companions: For a low grouping with color, plant Variegated Arboricola as the tallest layer, Dwarf Ixora in the middle, and border with Juniper or Fire Croton. For layered hedges, plant Viburnum or Lakeview Jasmine as the tallest layer, Silver Buttonwood in the middle, and border with Dwarf Ixora.

Dwarf Ixora and more companions

Care in the Landscape: Dwarf Ixora has a very compact growth habit, which only requires occasional trimming. Trim as needed, usually a few times per year, to maintain at the desired size. This small Ixora requires regular fertilization because its nutritional needs are high. Fertilize in March, June, and October with an acidic, slow-release fertilizer with minor elements. Minor elements, especially iron, play an important part in the health of this plant.

GROWING CONDITIONS

LIGHT: Light shade to full sun.

WATER: After initial establishment period, medium water. Ideal is once or twice a week. Tolerates irrigation up to 3 times a week. Untested without irrigation.

SOIL: Prefers a slightly acidic soil, but performs acceptably in south Florida native soils, so long as they are well drained.

SALT TOLERANCE: Medium

WIND TOLERANCE: Medium

ZONE: 10b to 11

PEST PROBLEMS: Scale

PROPAGATION: Cuttings

Botanical Name: *Juniperus chinensis 'Parsonii'*

Common Name: **Juniper Parsonii**

CHARACTERISTICS

PLANT TYPE: Groundcover

AVERAGE SIZE: 1 to 2 feet tall by about 2 feet wide.

GROWTH RATE: Medium

LEAF: Deep gray-green; dense and needlelike; about 1 inch long.

FLOWER: Insignificant

BEST COLOR: No seasonal variation.

AVERAGE LIFE: 10 to 15 years. May last only 5 years if watered more than once or twice a week. Lives longer in zone 10a than zone 10b.

ORIGIN: China

CAUTIONS: Do not overwater.

SPACING: 2 to 3 feet on center; if placed at 3 feet, Juniper plants will take about 2 years to fill in an area.

An easy groundcover with the northern look of an evergreen.

Juniper Parsonii as a border

General: This Juniper gives a northern look to the garden. It also adds texture, which is its primary benefit. It stays low with little trimming and requires very little water. Juniper is a fine edging plant and groundcover for large areas. Although Juniper does better further north than south in Florida, it is a valuable addition to our groundcover list because we have so few groundcovers available.

Podocarpus is a good companion for Juniper.

Companions: For a northern look, Juniper is a wonderful border for Podocarpus. Juniper also fits in well with manicured gardens. Companions for a manicured look include hedges like Lakeview Jasmine, Viburnum, Variegated Arboricola, and Silver Buttonwood. Flowering plants that look good with Juniper borders include Ixora Super King and Dwarf Ixora. Philodendron Xanadu and the Foxtail Fern are good companions for textural interest.

Juniper

Dwarf Ixora

Variegated Arboricola

Juniper and some companions

Care in the Landscape: The most common mistake made with Juniper is overwatering. It does not require much trimming, only to keep it within its desired bounds. Its nutritional needs are low, but it appreciates and grows faster from fertilization in March, June, and October with a well-balanced, slow-release mix with minor elements.

LIGHT: Full sun

WATER: After initial establishment period, low water. Ideal is once a week. Tolerates irrigation up to twice a week. Survives without irrigation in average environmental conditions.

SOIL: Wide range of well-drained soils; intolerant of wet soil.

SALT TOLERANCE: Medium

WIND TOLERANCE: Medium

ZONE: 4 to 10b. Tolerates temperatures to 0 deg.F. Does better in zone 10a and further north than in zone 10b, but is widely used in 10b.

PEST PROBLEMS: Mites. Fungus, if overwatered.

PROPAGATION: Cuttings

Botanical Name: *Juniperus conferta*

Common Name: **Shore Juniper**

CHARACTERISTICS

PLANT TYPE: Groundcover

AVERAGE SIZE: 6 to 12 inches tall by about 24 inches wide.

GROWTH RATE: Medium

LEAF: Tiny dark-green needles.

FLOWER: Inconspicuous cone.

BEST COLOR: No seasonal variation.

AVERAGE LIFE: 5 to 15 years.

ORIGIN: Japan

CAUTIONS: Do not overwater.

SPACING: 12 to 24 inches on center.

A low, almost flat groundcover with the look of a northern evergreen.

Shore Juniper cascading over the edge of a planter. This is an unusual use for Juniper, which is normally planted in the ground.

General: Shore Juniper is an easy groundcover that is lower than most south Florida plants. It requires very little care and is especially useful in high salt situations. Shore Juniper works well in rock gardens. It does best in the northern parts of south Florida, but it is also commonly used throughout the area. The photo above was taken in Boca Raton, where the Juniper had been living happily for a number of years.

Silver Buttonwood   *Ixora 'Super King'*

Some companions

Companions: For a northern look, Juniper is a wonderful groundcover around Podocarpus. Juniper also fits in well with manicured gardens. Companions for a manicured look include hedges like Lakeview Jasmine, Viburnum, Variegated Arboricola, and Silver Buttonwood. Flowering plants that look good with Juniper borders include Ixora Super King and Dwarf Ixora. Philodendron Xanadu and the Foxtail Fern are good companions for textural interest.

Shore Juniper with more companions

Care in the Landscape: This is a very easy plant. The most common mistake made with Juniper is overwatering. It does not require much trimming, only to keep it within its desired bounds. Its nutritional needs are low, but it appreciates and grows faster from fertilization in March, June, and October with a well-balanced, slow-release mix with minor elements.

GROWING CONDITIONS

LIGHT: Full sun

WATER: After initial establishment period, low water. Ideal is once a week. Tolerates irrigation up to twice a week. Survives without irrigation in average environmental conditions.

SOIL: Wide range, as long as it is well drained. This Juniper will not tolerate poorly drained, wet soil.

SALT TOLERANCE: High

WIND TOLERANCE: Medium

ZONE: 6 to 10b. Will tolerate all of Florida's freezes. Does best in zones 10a and further north, but is commonly used in zone 10b.

PEST PROBLEMS: Mites, but not as susceptible to mites as other varieties of Juniper.

PROPAGATION: Cuttings or seeds.

Botanical Name: *Liriope muscari 'Evergreen Giant'*

Common Name: **Liriope Evergreen Giant**

CHARACTERISTICS

PLANT TYPE: Groundcover

AVERAGE SIZE: Eventually grows to 3 feet tall by 2 feet wide. Most gardens feature Liriope in the 12 to 24 inch height range and remove it when it gets too tall.

GROWTH RATE: Slow

LEAF: Dark green; about 12 to 20 inches long by 1/4 inch wide; resembles grass.

FLOWER: Occasional purple spikes.

BEST COLOR: Insignificant flowers appear occasionally in summer, but this plant is grown for foliage, not flower color.

AVERAGE LIFE: Never seems to die of old age.

ORIGIN: Eastern Asia

CAUTIONS: Do not overwater.

SPACING: 12 to 24 inches on center.

One of the easiest and most versatile plants in south Florida. Great for borders or massing in sun or shade.

Variegated Liriope forms the front border, with Evergreen Giant Liriope in the middle. A Ficus hedge forms the tallest layer. Variegated Liriope, or Aztec Grass, is not as easy as Evergreen Giant Liriope. Aztec Grass frequently has brown tips on the leaves.

General: Liriope is among the toughest plants commonly available in south Florida. It takes extreme variations of light, from direct sun to deep shade. It thrives in wet or dry soils, provided it is not kept continually moist. Liriope requires absolutely no maintenance for about five years. The only negative about Liriope is that it is over-planted in many locations. Commonly, it is planted at about six inches tall and the owners do not realize that it cannot be maintained at that low height. After about ten years, it is three feet tall and towering over the layers behind it. However, if a plant gives ten years of use with minimal cost or care, it is definitely worth the price.

Companions: Liriope works very well as a border for paths or gardens with any type of plant material. Its style is neutral, working with tropical, manicured, or cottage gardens. The dark green color works with other greens, light colors, or bright colors.

A recently planted Evergreen Giant Liriope

Care in the Landscape: Liriope is not a heavy feeder. If the plant turns light green or yellowish all over, it is suffering from nutritional deficiencies and needs feeding. For best care, fertilize in March, June, and October with a well-balanced, slow-release mix with minor elements. Liriope can be trimmed occasionally. It recovers fastest if trimmed hard in March. The plant will look like it had a crew cut for a few months, which is a good reason to only trim about once every five years. Liriope can also be thinned. This is best done with a very sharp shovel. The shovel can be sharpened with an electric grinder. Cut away unwanted portions of the plant with the shovel and transplant it elsewhere or give it to a friend.

LIGHT: Dense shade to full sun.

WATER: After initial establishment period, low water. Ideal is once a week. Tolerates irrigation up to twice a week. Survives without irrigation in average environmental conditions.

SOIL: Wide range

SALT TOLERANCE: Medium

WIND TOLERANCE: High

ZONE: 6 to 10b

PEST PROBLEMS: None serious; if some of the leaves turn yellow while most of the leaves remain green, the plant has fungus. Spray if serious and cut back on water.

PROPAGATION: Tissue culture, division.

Botanical Name: *Microsorum scolopendrium*

Common Name: **Wart Fern**

CHARACTERISTICS

PLANT TYPE: Groundcover

AVERAGE SIZE: 2 feet tall by 1 1/2 to 2 feet wide.

GROWTH RATE: Medium

LEAF: Dark green; about 12 to 16 inches long at maturity.

FLOWER: None

BEST COLOR: No seasonal variation.

AVERAGE LIFE: Unknown. Thought to be 10 to 20 years.

ORIGIN: Pacific basin

CAUTIONS: None known

SPACING: 18 inches on center.

A lush, tropical plant that covers the ground beautifully. Under-used in south Florida.

Wart Ferns planted in a mass

General: Wart Fern is a beautiful groundcover for shady areas. It is quite different from what most people think of as ferns because its leaf is much wider and lusher. Its unique appearance fits into many different styles. Its compact growth habit works well in manicured gardens, while its woodland feel is appropriate in informal gardens as well. This fern is much easier to keep within bounds than the more common Sword Fern.

Perfection Bromeliad *Dwarf Chenille* *Petra Croton*

Some companions

Companions: Wart Fern works well with most of the shade plants in this book. One good combination is Wart Ferns with Perfection Bromeliads, Dwarf Chenilles, and Petra Crotons. Ti Red Sisters and Sanchezias work well in the same mix. A shade cottage garden could include Wart Ferns with Angelwing Begonias, Shrimp Plants, Yellow Mussaendas, and Mend Bromeliads.

Wart Fern

Ti Red Sister

Sanchezia

Wart Fern with more companions

Care in the Landscape: Wart Ferns are very easy to grow. Fertilize in March, June, and October with a well-balanced, slow-release mix that contains minor elements. They require less fertilizer in shade situations under trees if the leaves are allowed to break down into mulch underneath them. Most of my experiences with Wart Ferns have been in the last five years, so I am not familiar with any other problems that might crop up beyond that time.

Botanical Name: *Neoregelia 'Perfection'* *cv. of Fosperior (variegated)*

Common Name: **Perfection Bromeliad**

CHARACTERISTICS

PLANT TYPE: Groundcover

AVERAGE SIZE: 6 to 12 inches tall by 24 to 30 inches wide.

GROWTH RATE: Slow

LEAF: Burgundy, black, and cream stripes; about 12 to 18 inches long with spines along the edges.

FLOWER: Tiny purple flowers appear in the center well in spring. The flowers are insignificant. Use this plant for leaf color.

BEST COLOR: No seasonal variation.

AVERAGE LIFE: Single plant lives about 2 years but sends up babies to replace itself. A clump of good landscape bromeliads lasts indefinitely.

ORIGIN: Tropical America

CAUTIONS: Leaves have spines. Wear long sleeves and gloves when handling.

SPACING: 2 feet on center

An ideal landscape plant offering constant color in partial sun or shade. Requires trimming only once a year.

The Perfection Bromeliad does well when planted in the ground, in pots, or mounted on trees.

General: The Perfection Bromeliad is a strong landscape bromeliad. It has a dramatic appearance and is one of the few subtropical groundcovers that stays under 12 inches. This bromeliad takes more sun than most.

Perfection and Mend Bromeliads add definition to this garden.

Companions: Use the Perfection Bromeliad as an accent plant in partially sunny or shady areas. It combines well with other Bromeliads, especially the Mend Bromeliad. Other excellent companions include Ti Plants, Crotons, Wart Ferns, and Dwarf Chenilles. Perfection Bromeliads look good planted as ground-cover around rocks. Light colored gravels, like off-white river rock, show off the dark colors of the leaves.

Perfection Bromeliads make a dramatic statement when massed together. Dwarf Mondo grass surrounds the stepping stones, from which I had poor results in my trials. Although it did well in some locations, it did poorly in others with no apparent reason.

Care in the Landscape: The mother plant dies after flowering and producing pups (babies). Trim off the dead plant after it becomes brown. Leave the remaining pups (babies) to grow where they are or separate them to cover more ground. Do this about once a year. Bromeliads do not require regular fertilization. If faster growth is desired, fertilize in March, June, and October with a well-balanced, slow-release mix that contains minor ele-ments. Do not apply fertilizer to the center well of the plant.

Botanical Name: *Nephrolepis biserrata 'Furcans'*

Common Name: **Fishtail Fern**

CHARACTERISTICS

PLANT TYPE: Groundcover

AVERAGE SIZE: 2 to 3 feet tall by 2 to 3 feet wide.

GROWTH RATE: Medium

LEAF: Medium green; 3 to 4 inches wide by about 2 feet long. Leaf tips look like fishtails.

FLOWER: None

BEST COLOR: No seasonal variation.

AVERAGE LIFE: 10 to 15 years.

ORIGIN: Tropical America

CAUTIONS: None known

SPACING: 3 feet on center. While plants seem too far apart on planting day, they fill in quickly.

An excellent low maintenance, inexpensive groundcover for areas too shady for grass.

Before

Before, the grass was thinning because of too much shade.

General: The Fishtail Fern is one of the best ferns available. Most other ferns for south Florida are invasive, meaning they spread too aggressively. The Fishtail Fern is much easier to control. It is an excellent choice for areas too shady for grass because it is low maintenance and inexpensive. Be sure to plant it three feet on center to take advantage of its low cost per square foot. If planted any closer, the plant has a higher chance of developing fungus. It fills in quickly.

Companions: Fishtail Ferns make wonderful woodland gardens. Combine with Ti Plants and Crotons for a bold look. For a wildflower look, combine with Shrimp Plants, Angelwing Begonias, Ruellia Purple Showers, and Starburst Pentas.

After

After, Fishtail Ferns transform this garden.

Care in the Landscape: The Fishtail Fern requires almost no care. It seldom needs fertilization to maintain health. If faster growth is desired or a nutritional deficiency is noticed, fertilize with a well-balanced, slow-release mix that includes minor elements. Trim off any dead fronds that appear from time to time. If the ferns look leggy or overgrown, trim to about six inches tall. Trim in summer for faster recovery.

Botanical Name: *Pentas lanceolata 'Starburst'*

Common Name: **Starburst Pentas**

CHARACTERISTICS

PLANT TYPE: Groundcover

AVERAGE SIZE: Easily maintained at sizes between 2 feet tall by 18 inches wide and 3 feet tall by 2 feet wide.

GROWTH RATE: Fast

LEAF: Medium green, pointed; 2 to 3 inches long.

FLOWER: 2 to 3 inch clusters of small, star-shaped flowers. Bright pink and pale pink but, from a distance, seem medium pink.

BEST COLOR: All year

AVERAGE LIFE: 2 to 3 years.

ORIGIN: Tropical Africa

CAUTIONS: None known

SPACING: 18 inches on center for a tight look; 24 for a natural look.

An excellent older variety that lives longer than most Pentas. Blooms better in shade than any of the other Pentas.

Starburst Pentas planted in a mass

General: Starburst Pentas bloom constantly with very little care. They are much tougher than many of the newer Pentas. Their semi-dwarf form requires little trimming, and the bicolor flower is unique. This is the best Pentas for cut flowers and, like all Pentas, is an excellent butterfly attracter. The Starburst Pentas live longer than the newer hybrid Pentas - a full two to three years - which makes them much more economical than annuals. The newer, 'New Look' series of Pentas are smaller than the Starburst. They are also much shorter lived, lasting for about six months. Although the Starburst Pentas thrive in full sun, they are the best Pentas for light to medium shade situations.

Companions: Starburst Pentas look good with most of the plants in this book. For easy color in sun, plant Firespike as the tallest layer, then Thryallis, and border with Starburst Pentas. For a low garden in shade, plant Walking Iris as the tallest layer, then Starburst Pentas, and border with Blue Daze. Starburst Pentas are also good with Mend Bromeliads.

Starburst Pentas and some companions

Care in the Landscape: Fertilize in March, June, and October with a well-balanced, slow-release mix that contains minor elements. For a natural look, trim twice a year. For a compact look, machine-shear six times a year to the desired size. Starburst Pentas benefit from hard pruning (to about 8 to 12 inches) in July to promote air circulation through the plant for fungal control during rainy months.

Botanical Name: *Ruellia brittoniana 'Compacta Katie'*

Common Name: **Mexican Bluebell, Ruellia Katie**

CHARACTERISTICS

PLANT TYPE: Groundcover

AVERAGE SIZE: 6 to 12 inches tall by 6 to 12 inches wide.

GROWTH RATE: Medium

LEAF: Spear-like, dark green; about 4 to 6 inches long.

FLOWER: Purple, pink, or white bell about 1 1/2 inches wide.

BEST COLOR: Spring through fall; flowers through quite a bit of the winter if the temperature stays warm. Stops flowering for a few months in the average winter.

AVERAGE LIFE: 5 years

ORIGIN: Mexico

CAUTIONS: Reseeds

SPACING: 8 to 18 inches on center.

Note: Ruellia Katie did fairly well in the landscape in 1999 through 2000. It has not done so well in 2001 and 2002. I am not sure of its future as a landscape plant and am watching it closely.

An unusual, low growing groundcover that lasts for years and blooms most of the time. Some problems in 2000 and 2001 (see "Note" below).

Ruellia Katie growing in front of Mend Bromeliads, Shrimp Plants, and Angelwing Begonias.

General: Ruellia Katie is useful primarily because of its size, long bloom period, and ease of care. Most subtropical landscape plants grow much larger than the Ruellia Katie's one foot height. It does reseed sometimes, enough to be a nuisance. Removing the unwanted seedlings occasionally is much easier than constantly trimming or replacing the plant. Ruellia Katie has been available for years in purple. Pink and white are recent introductions. I have only been testing these new colors for about a year. Ruellia Purple Showers is a much taller Ruellia with the same purple flower. It is covered on pages 108 and 109.

Companions: Ruellia makes an excellent border for flowering shrubs. Use one color or alternate purple, white, and pink. For an easy garden in partial shade, plant Angelwing Begonias as the tallest layer, then Shrimps, then Ruellias. This shade arrangement is shown opposite. In sun, try Ruellia as a border for Shrimp Plants and Cranberry Pentas.

Purple Ruellia Katie

Pink Ruellia Katie

White Ruellia Katie

The three colors of Ruellia Katie

Care in the Landscape: Fertilize in March, June, and October with a well-balanced, slow-release mix that contains minor elements. To encourage full growth, nip the ends of the stems if they look leggy. The plants spread and need thinning or separating every five years or so.

Botanical Name: *Spathoglottis plicata*

Common Name: **Ground Orchid, Garden Orchid**

CHARACTERISTICS

PLANT TYPE: Groundcover

AVERAGE SIZE: 2 feet tall by 2 feet wide.

GROWTH RATE: Medium

LEAF: Medium green; about 1 to 2 feet long.

FLOWER: Lavender, yellow or dark purple. Flowers measure about 1 inch across.

BEST COLOR: Flowers 8 to 10 months of the year on the average. Blooms peak in spring, summer, and fall. Stops blooming in winter for a few months.

AVERAGE LIFE: Unknown, but at least 5 years.

ORIGIN: Far East and Australia.

CAUTIONS: None known

SPACING: 18 inches on center.

Finally... an easy Orchid that grows in the garden among the other flowers and blooms most of the year.

Recently planted Garden Orchids

General: Orchids are the world's favorite flowers and are traditionally thought of as difficult to grow. Garden Orchids are the exception, blooming for most of the year with minimal care. The flowers are not as large as those on the showy Cattleya Orchids, but the profusion of blooms makes a great show in the garden. Most orchids grow in trees and require different treatment than plants that grow in the ground. Garden Orchids grow in the ground, requiring similar care to other flowering plants. Their one drawback is leaf yellowing in the winter.

Companions: Do not put this plant in an area where it will be a focal point in the winter, as it may get yellow leaves with cool weather. Very adaptable to different landscape styles, Garden Orchids look good in tropical, manicured, or cottage gardens. They also are excellent specimens for pots. Some flowering plants that look especially nice with Garden Orchids include Thryallis, Shrimp Plants, Cranberry Pentas, and Yellow Mussaendas.

A mature clump of Garden Orchids photographed in fall

Care in the Landscape: Fertilize Garden Orchids in March, June, and October with a well-balanced, slow-release mix that contains minor elements. Trim to remove brown leaves. This plant normally has some brown portions on the leaves, as shown in the opposite photo. These need not be removed unless they become an eyesore. In the winter, quite a few leaves turn yellow. Remove them as needed. This is a very easy plant and only occasionally requires attention.

GROWING CONDITIONS

LIGHT: Medium shade to full sun. The ideal light is partial sun, partial shade, but the plant performs acceptably in a full sun environment.

WATER: After initial establishment period, medium water. Ideal is once or twice a week in shade or twice a week in sun. Tolerates irrigation up to 3 times a week. Untested without irrigation.

SOIL: Wide range

SALT TOLERANCE: Unknown

WIND TOLERANCE: Unknown

ZONE: 10b to 11

PEST PROBLEMS: None serious. It is normal for leaves to brown occasionally.

PROPAGATION: Division of clumps.

NOTES: I have tested 4 different Ground Orchids. The Grapette, which is a smaller variety with darker purple flowers, is a beautiful plant. However, its cold tolerance is nowhere near as good as the larger, light purple variety. I lost all my Grapettes in the winter of 1995. I am currently testing a lovely yellow and another with white, purple, and yellow on the same flower. I have high hopes for these two but do not have enough experience with them yet to recommend them.

Botanical Name: *Tradescantia pallida 'Purpurea'*

Common Name: **Purple Queen**

CHARACTERISTICS

PLANT TYPE: Groundcover

AVERAGE SIZE: Easily maintained at sizes between 6 to 12 inches tall by 12 to 24 inches wide.

GROWTH RATE: Medium

LEAF: Purple; about 1 inch wide by 3 inches long.

FLOWER: About 1/2 inch in diameter; rather insignificant, light purple. Use this plant for its leaf color.

BEST COLOR: No seasonal variation. Blooms sporadically throughout the warm months, but most of the color is from the leaves.

AVERAGE LIFE: 1 to 3 years. Lasts longer in a low water environment.

ORIGIN: Mexico

CAUTIONS: Sap is a skin irritant. Brittle, so the stems often break while planting. However, broken stems will take root if planted, even if they are unrooted.

SPACING: 12 to 18 inches on center is average. 6 inches for faster coverage.

Dramatic color from a groundcover that stays lower than most.

Purple Queen is between Shrimps and Crown of Thorns. If the arrangement was not on a hill, the Crown of Thorns would outgrow the Purple Queen.

General: Purple Queen makes a strong statement for those who like purple. It is excellent in difficult environments, particularly high salt environments or pots. It is best viewed from a distance because of a rather messy appearance up close. Although short-lived, it is much more economical than annuals.

Companions: Purple Queen contrasts well with plants that have silver leaves, such as Bismarckia Palms, Silver Buttonwoods, and Palmettos. These also work well in medium salt situations. Other plants that work with Purple Queens in salty areas include Ixoras, Crotons, Variegated Arboricolas, and Crown of Thorns.

Bands of color are formed by yellow Shrimp Plants, Cranberry Pentas, and a border of Purple Queen.

Care in the Landscape: Fertilize in March, June, and October with a well-balanced, slow-release mix that contains minor elements. Trim to groom the plant, so it does not become leggy and uneven.

LIGHT: Light shade to full sun. Performs badly in too much shade.

WATER: After initial establishment period, low water. Ideal is once a week. Tolerates irrigation up to twice a week. Survives without irrigation in average environmental conditions.

SOIL: Wide range

SALT TOLERANCE: High

WIND TOLERANCE: High

ZONE: 9 to 11. Damaged by frost but recovers with warm weather.

PEST PROBLEMS: Fungus

PROPAGATION: Roots very easily from cuttings.

Botanical Name: *Trimezia martinicensis*

Common Name: **Walking Iris**

CHARACTERISTICS

PLANT TYPE: Groundcover

AVERAGE SIZE: 2 feet tall by 2 feet wide.

GROWTH RATE: Medium

LEAF: Medium green; about 24 inches long by 1 inch wide.

FLOWER: Yellow, orchid-like bloom about 2 inches across. Opens only in daytime.

BEST COLOR: Flowers appear on and off all year. This plant blooms about 80% of the year.

AVERAGE LIFE: 10 years

ORIGIN: Tropical America

CAUTIONS: None known

SPACING: 18 inches on center.

Great plant for lovely flowers and vertical texture in either sun or deep shade. Deserves much more use in south Florida.

Recently planted Walking Iris

General: The first time I saw a Walking Iris, I thought it was an orchid and probably hard to grow. I was wrong on both counts. The flower is unique, resembling an Orchid, but is actually a subtropical iris. And the plant is simple to grow. The Walking Iris blooms in deep shade, a quality shared by few other plants. I tested many irises and, while all the others had a very short bloom period, the Walking Iris blooms most of the time.

Companions: For a garden in deep shade, combine the Iris with ferns and palms. A woodland garden in medium shade could include the Iris with the Angelwing Begonia, Yellow Mussaenda, Starburst Pentas and Blue Daze.

Close-up of Iris flower

Care in the Landscape: Fertilize in March, June, and October with a well-balanced, slow-release mix that contains minor elements. If the plant turns yellowish all over, it needs more fertilizer. Groom the plant from time to time to remove any brown leaves. Every few years, divide the clumps of Iris by taking the whole mass out of the ground, breaking it up into smaller pieces, and planting a few small ones. Spread the others out in other places or give to a friend. If plants are not periodically divided (every two or three years), they look quite messy.

Botanical Name: *Tripsacum floridana*

Common Name: **Dwarf Fakahatchee Grass, Florida Gama Grass**

CHARACTERISTICS

PLANT TYPE: Groundcover

AVERAGE SIZE: 2 feet tall by 2 feet wide.

GROWTH RATE: Medium

LEAF: Medium green; about 18 inches long by 1/2 inch wide.

FLOWER: Long, plume-like flower in fall. Not significant for its color, but adds an interesting texture.

BEST COLOR: No significant seasonal variation. Subtle color from fall bloom.

AVERAGE LIFE: At least 5 years.

ORIGIN: South Florida

CAUTIONS: None known

SPACING: 12 to 24 inches on center.

One of the toughest native groundcovers available in south Florida. A good source of fine texture.

Dwarf Fakahatchee Grass looks better from a distance (opposite) than it does up close (above).

General: Dwarf Fakahatchee is a short, dense groundcover that is becoming more popular in south Florida, especially in street plantings and along golf courses. It is better used in large masses viewed from a distance rather than up close. The main benefit of the plant is its light texture and durability in the landscape.

Left: Another Fakahatchee Grass (Tripsacum dactyloides) is more common in the trade but not as attractive. It is larger and has a coarser texture, lacking the graceful look of the Dwarf Fakahatchee.

Companions: Dwarf Fakahatchee works beautifully with coarse-textured natives, like Sabal Palms, Palmettos, and Thatch Palms. Native shrubs that look good with this grass include Firebush and Cocoplum. Gumbo Limbo is a great tree companion.

Dwarf Fakahatchee Grass in the landscape

Care in the Landscape: Dwarf Fakahatchee Grass is easy to grow. Fertilize in March, June, and October with a well-balanced, slow-release mix with minor elements. If the weather is too cold or the soil too dry, the leaves brown. Cut the plant back once a year in summer. This cutback not only removes dead leaves but also gives space for removing any weeds growing under the plant. The plant recovers quickly from severe cutbacks in about three to four weeks, if done in summer.

GROWING CONDITIONS

LIGHT: Light shade to full sun.

WATER: After initial establishment period, medium water. Ideal is twice a week. Tolerates irrigation every day. Untested without irrigation.

SOIL: Wide range

SALT TOLERANCE: Medium

WIND TOLERANCE: Unknown

ZONE: 7 to 11; leaves brown if farther north than zone 10 in winter.

PEST PROBLEMS: None known.

PROPAGATION: Seeds, division.

CHAPTER 2

SHRUBS, 2 TO 8 FEET TALL

Pictured left: Shrub layers with Ruellia Purple Showers in the back, Yellow Mussaenda in the middle, and Cranberry Pentas in front. Above: Yellow Mussaenda flower.

Botanical Name: *Acalypha wilkesiana 'Godseffiana'*

Common Name: **Curly Ruffle**

CHARACTERISTICS

PLANT TYPE: Shrub

AVERAGE SIZE: Easily maintained at sizes between 4 feet tall by 2 feet wide and 8 feet tall by 3 feet wide.

GROWTH RATE: Fast

LEAF: Green with a white edge; 3 to 4 inches wide.

FLOWER: Inconspicuous

BEST COLOR: No seasonal variation.

AVERAGE LIFE: At least 10 years.

ORIGIN: East Indies

CAUTIONS: None known

SPACING: 2 to 3 feet on center.

Use this unique, old Florida plant for its interesting texture. The edges of the curled leaves resemble rickrack.

The Curly Ruffle is the tallest layer, bordered by Shrimps.

General: This is an old Florida plant I found years ago in Miami that merits attention. The interesting, curly leaf shape with white edges is the main benefit. The Curly Ruffle is very easy to grow, provided it is maintained at a minimum of four feet tall. Use the Curly Ruffle in cottage gardens or tropical gardens, either as a specimen or mass. Plant other layers in front of the Curly Ruffle to hide its bare base.

Jatropha   *Sanchezia*   *Mammey Croton*

Some companions

Ti Red Sister   Shrimp Plant   Petra Croton   Dwarf Chenille

Other companions

Companions: For a tropical look, plant the Curly Ruffles among Palms and large-leafed plants, like the White Bird of Paradise. The color of the Curly Ruffle shows well accented with plants that have bright leaf colors or flowers, such as Crotons, Jatrophas, Shrimp Plants, Ti Plants or Dwarf Chenilles. Avoid plants with pale flowers, such as Plumbago, because pales wash out with the Curly Ruffle's light green and white coloration.

Close-up of the leaf. The leaves are larger than shown.

Care in the Landscape: Fertilize in March, June, and October with a well-balanced, slow-release mix that contains minor elements. Trim to maintain the desired height - about once a year for a height of eight to twelve feet, twice a year for five to eight feet, and at least three times a year for three to five feet. The Curly Ruffle recovers quickly from aggressive cutbacks (in about a month) if trimmed from April to September. Cut the side branches as well as the top, as the plant has a tendency to become leggy. The Curly Ruffle is much easier to maintain if its desired height is at least five feet, and it is bordered by one or two layers of shorter plants in front.

GROWING CONDITIONS

LIGHT: Full sun. This plant looks best in very bright light. Less compact in shade.

WATER: After initial establishment period, medium water. Ideal is twice a week. Tolerates irrigation up to 3 times per week. Untested without irrigation.

SOIL: Wide range

SALT TOLERANCE: Medium

WIND TOLERANCE: Medium

ZONE: 10b to 11. Loses its curly texture when it experiences too much cold.

PEST PROBLEMS: I have never seen any pests on this plant in a nursery situation or in the landscape. I have heard of occasional infestations with mealybugs.

PROPAGATION: Cuttings

Botanical Name: *Allamanda schottii*

Common Name: **Shrub or Bush Allamanda**

CHARACTERISTICS

PLANT TYPE: Shrub

AVERAGE SIZE: Easily maintained at sizes between 3 feet tall by 2 feet wide to 5 feet tall by 3 feet wide. Seldom flowers if kept shorter than three feet.

GROWTH RATE: Medium

LEAF: Green, pointed; 2 to 3 inches long.

FLOWER: Trumpet shaped, yellow; about 2 inches long.

BEST COLOR: Flowers about half the year with blooms appearing spring, summer, and fall. Bloom time varies from year to year, based on average temperature.

AVERAGE LIFE: 10 years

ORIGIN: South America

CAUTIONS: None known. Not poisonous like the vine Allamanda.

SPACING: 2 feet on center for a tight look; 3 feet, for an unstructured, natural appearance.

A tough shrub that has been grown here for many years. The flower resembles a Daffodil.

The taller shrub with the yellow flowers is the Allamanda. The placement of the Allamanda is appropriate - as a middle layer.

General: Shrub Allamanda has been popular for many years because of its attractive yellow flower and dark green, shiny leaves. Because it has a tendency towards legginess, use it as a middle or back layer in an informal garden. If it is used as a front layer, the unattractive, bare lower branches will show. Shrub Allamanda is frequently trimmed too short to flower significantly. Keep it at least three feet tall for adequate flowering.

Companions: Shrub Allamanda does not have enough impact to use alone or with other green plants. Use it with colorful plants. It fits well in a cottage garden or a tropical garden, combining nicely with most other flowering plants. It does not shear well into a hedge. Use taller plants behind it, like Blue Butterfly or Jatropha. Plant a border in front to hide its bottom branches, which are naturally bare. Border suggestions include Plumbago, Pentas, or Blue Porterflower.

Close up of the Allamanda flower

Care in the Landscape: Shrub Allamanda is a medium feeder. Fertilize in March, June, and October with a well-balanced, slow-release mix that contains minor elements. If you occasionally forget, the plant will survive, possibly suffering some overall yellowing of the leaves. Occasional hand pruning is the key to its success in the landscape. This plant requires hand pruning and will not be an acceptable landscape plant for long without it. If continually machine-sheared, it stops blooming. Hand-prune one to three times per year, depending on the size you want to maintain. The smaller you want it, the more you need to trim it. Be sure to trim the side branches as well as the top. Trim while the plant is taking a rest from blooming. Shrub Allamanda responds very well to very hard cutbacks in the summer. Or, stagger cut (prune one third of the tallest branches to the ground) several times a year.

GROWING CONDITIONS

LIGHT: Light shade to full sun. Flowers more in full sun.

WATER: Requires a medium amount of water once it is established. Needs more than average water for the first few months after planting. It signals this need by wilting and the lower leaves turning yellow. Should this occur, give the plant more water and understand that the need for excessive amounts of water abates after establishment. Ideal water is twice a week. Tolerates irrigation up to 3 times a week. Untested without irrigation.

SOIL: Wide range

SALT TOLERANCE: Medium

WIND TOLERANCE: Medium

ZONE: 10a to 11

PEST PROBLEMS: None serious.

PROPAGATION: Cuttings

NOTES: Do not confuse Shrub Allamanda with vine Allamanda. Its flower is smaller than that of the vine Allamanda. It is much easier to control and less likely to suffer from chlorosis, a deficiency of green pigment caused by lack of nutrients. Vine Allamanda is poisonous. Shrub Allamanda is not.

Botanical Name: *Begonia flamingo* (also known as Begonia coccinea pink and Begonia 'Di-Erna')

Common Name: **Pink Angelwing Begonia**

CHARACTERISTICS

PLANT TYPE: Shrub

AVERAGE SIZE: Easily maintained at sizes between 3 feet tall by 2 feet wide and 7 feet tall by 3 feet wide.

GROWTH RATE: Medium

LEAF: Green and shaped like the wing of an angel; about 3 to 4 inches long.

FLOWER: Very showy pink clusters about 5 inches across.

BEST COLOR: Blooms all year. Peaks in winter.

AVERAGE LIFE: At least 10 years.

ORIGIN: Many Angelwing Begonias are native to Brazil. The exact origin of this cultivar is unknown.

CAUTIONS: None known

SPACING: 2 to 3 feet on center.

NOTE: Many types of Angelwing Begonias exist. They are available in several different flower colors, some with solid green leaves and some with interesting leaf patterns. I have tried many and have found no other yet that offers the length of bloom time and long life span of this one. However, my trials continue. There is much confusion in the trade regarding the name of this plant. Take a picture to be sure of buying this one.

The most spectacular shade plant in this book. This perennial Begonia blooms every day of the year with large, beautiful hanging clusters of pink flowers. It lives for over ten years.

This specimen is eight years old. It blooms constantly and is five feet tall.

General: I have tested about 2500 different plants. The Pink Angelwing Begonia is the best plant I tested. It blooms every day of the year in shade, which is very unusual. Large specimens add instant color and impact to a garden and are very easy to grow. Angelwing Begonias are informal plants, perfect for tropical or cottage gardens. Use this Begonia as a mass or an accent. It is perfect for accenting the front of a house, particularly between windows.

Do not confuse this Begonia with the small annual Begonias that only last one season. This one is a perennial and lives for many years. It grows quite large, as shown left. The Pink Angelwing Begonia is quite beautiful, and a must for every south Florida shade garden.

Note: This Begonia gives more impact as it grows. If you purchase one in a small, three gallon pot, it will need six months to a year to give much impact. For an immediate effect, plant larger plants in seven to twenty-five gallon nursery pots.

Companions: In a tropical landscape, Begonias layer well with Bromeliads, Tis, and Caricature Plants. In a cottage garden, they mix compatibly with Ground Orchids, Blue Porterflowers, Yellow Mussaendas, and Shrimp Plants.

The flower of the Angelwing Begonia is about this size when the plant is mature but is smaller when the plant is young. It is quite beautiful and shows well up close or at a distance.

Care in the Landscape: Fertilize your Begonias in March, June, and October with a well-balanced, slow-release mix that contains minor elements. If the leaves yellow (all over) at any other time of the year, fertilize again, making sure that the fertilizer includes minor elements. The plant frequently is more yellow in hotter weather. Be sure to fertilize it enough to green it up. Trim any time of the year. Some prefer to even out the height of the different canes for a streamlined look. Others like the informal look of the plant's natural character, which is varying heights in the same plant. Branches will droop when the plant is too tall. Stake them if you want the height or cut the drooping branch to the ground. It will regrow from the base, filling in the bottom of the plant. As the plant matures, the canes thicken and support more height. If the plant looks bad in summer with leaf loss, brown spots on leaves, and general yellowing, renovate it by cutting it way back and fertilizing heavily.

LIGHT: Medium to light shade, not dense shade. Endures more light than you may think but not direct sun all day. Takes more sun in winter than summer.

WATER: After initial establishment period, low water. Ideal is once a week in medium shade, a bit more in more sun. Tolerates irrigation up to twice a week. Untested without irrigation.

SOIL: Wide range, if well drained.

SALT TOLERANCE: Low

WIND TOLERANCE: Untested

ZONE: 10a to 11. In 10 years, I have never seen any cold damage on this plant as far north as Jupiter.

PEST PROBLEMS: Fungus, shown by brown spots on the leaves. Cut back on water or spray with a fungicide if spots become severe. The spots appear in every rainy season. I have seldom found them offensive enough to spray except after very rainy periods. If a whole stalk goes black, cut several of them lengthwise and look for tiny white caterpillars. If you see them, spray with Orthene or equivalent. Occasional nematodes.

PROPAGATION: Roots quite easily from cuttings.

Botanical Name: *Breynia disticha*

Common Name: **Snowbush**

CHARACTERISTICS

PLANT TYPE: Shrub or small tree. See pages 134 and 135 for information on small tree.

AVERAGE SIZE: Easily maintained at sizes between 2 feet tall by 1 1/2 feet wide and 8 feet tall by 3 feet wide.

GROWTH RATE: Medium

LEAF: Small (about 1/2 inch) and multicolored in shades of pink, red, green, and white.

FLOWER: Insignificant

BEST COLOR: All year, but winter can cause the leaves to darken somewhat. Brighter in summer.

AVERAGE LIFE: 10 to 20 years.

ORIGIN: Pacific Islands

CAUTIONS: Sends out shoots that are a slight nuisance. Pull them out at least once a year. Severe, widespread caterpillar infestations occurred in 2000. See PEST PROBLEMS on opposite page.

SPACING: 18 to 24 inches on center.

One of south Florida's most decorative shrubs, adding long term color and texture to the garden.

Snowbush is the light-colored shrub in the middle of this garden. Notice how well it contrasts with the dark green hedge behind it and the hot pink of the Dwarf Bougainvillea in front.

General: This shrub is called Snowbush because its leaves resemble snow. It is best used (in shrub form) as a mass rather than a specimen. Snowbush is much thicker after it has been in the ground at least three to six months. It usually looks rather scrawny in nursery pots. I hesitated to use it for many years because I had heard it was invasive, producing so many runners that it became a nuisance. Extensive experience has shown me otherwise. It does send out runners but not enough to become a problem, provided you pull them out at least once a year.

Seminole Pink Hibiscus | Pinwheel Jasmine | Cranberry Pentas

Some companions

Companions: Snowbush combines beautifully with plants that have white or pink to red flowers. Use it as a middle layer, with Pinwheel Jasmine behind it and Cranberry Pentas in front. The Snowbush might outgrow the Pinwheel Jasmine at first. Keep it trimmed lower than the Jasmine until the Jasmine catches up. The Jasmine is a taller plant in the long run. Snowbush is also very attractive with Ti Red Sister as an accent and bordered with Liriope. Firespike and Hibiscus are attractive background plants surrounded by Snowbush.

Close-up of Snowbush leaves

Care in the Landscape: Snowbush is very easy to maintain. Fertilize in March, June, and October with a well-balanced, slow-release mix that contains minor elements. Trim as needed to control size. Snowbush can be machine-sheared as long as it gets a good hand pruning at least once a year. Trim some of the tallest branches to the ground to keep it full from the base.

GROWING CONDITIONS

LIGHT: Full sun. More colorful and dense in high light. Fades completely in shade.

WATER: After initial establishment period, medium water. Ideal is once or twice a week. Tolerates irrigation up to 4 times a week. Untested without irrigation.

SOIL: Wide range

SALT TOLERANCE: Medium

WIND TOLERANCE: Medium

ZONE: 10b to 11. Survives 32 deg. F. Foliage darkens and its brightness fades somewhat in response to temperatures under about 42 deg. F.

PEST PROBLEMS: At the time of writing this book, I question Snowbush as a low maintenance plant because of severe caterpillar infestations. During the 90's, I only witnessed occasional caterpillar attacks. In the summer of 2000, I heard of many. These attacks are severe enough to completely defoliate the plant. The caterpillar is easily controlled by spraying, but the plants in this book are relatively pest- resistant naturally. I include Snowbush in this book with the hope that the frequency of the attacks is an exception and not the norm.

PROPAGATION: Cuttings, runners.

Botanical Name: *Calliandra haematocephala 'Nana'*

Common Name: **Dwarf Powderpuff**

One of the easiest plants in this book. Blooms in sun or shade. Although the flower is small, the percentage of color is high.

Dwarf Powderpuff in full bloom. It takes about three years for this plant to reach this size from a three gallon nursery pot.

General: The Dwarf Powderpuff is one of the easiest and most dependable subtropical flowering shrubs. It flowers almost all the time in either sun or shade with very little care. The flower looks like a powderpuff and is nice to touch. Some say it resembles a Bottlebrush, but it is no relation. There is a larger Powderpuff that grows into a tree, but it does not flower anywhere near as often as the dwarf. The larger Powderpuff is also more susceptible to pests than the dwarf. The Dwarf Powderpuff can be deceptive, however, because it seldom looks good in a nursery pot. It will establish after about a month in the ground.

Some companions

Companions: The Dwarf Powderpuff combines well with fine or coarse textured plants. For a cottage garden look in the shade, alternate three Dwarf Powderpuffs with three Shrimp Plants and three Blue Porterflowers. Border with Dwarf Chenille. For a tropical look in shade, use Dwarf Powderpuff as an accent for White Birds of Paradise or Crotons. In sun, it works beautifully with Plumbago and Thryallis.

Close-up of the Dwarf Powderpuff flower; note the bud in the lower left corner that looks like a raspberry.

Care in the Landscape: The Dwarf Powderpuff is one of the easiest plants in this book. Fertilize it, if you remember. It might not notice, if you forget. Trim occasionally to maintain the desired size. For a natural look, this plant can go years without trimming.

GROWING CONDITIONS

LIGHT: Medium shade to full sun. This plant is extremely adaptable to different light conditions. It does not take dense shade.

WATER: After initial establishment period, low water. Ideal is once a week. Tolerates irrigation up to 3 times a week. Needs more than average water immediately after planting but not after it is well established in the landscape. Untested without irrigation.

SOIL: Wide range

SALT TOLERANCE: Low

WIND TOLERANCE: Low

ZONE: 10a to 11. Survives 30 deg. F. Looks poorly after cold weather but recovers quickly after it warms up.

PEST PROBLEMS: None known.

PROPAGATION: Seeds or cuttings.

Botanical Name: *Chrysobalanus icaco 'Red Tip'*

Common Name: **Red Tip Cocoplum**

CHARACTERISTICS

PLANT TYPE: Shrub

AVERAGE SIZE: Easily maintained at sizes between 3 feet tall by 2 feet wide and 12 feet tall by 10 feet wide. Most commonly used in the 3 foot range.

GROWTH RATE: Medium

LEAF: Medium to dark green or reddish brown; 1 to 2 inches long.

FLOWER: Insignificant

BEST COLOR: No seasonal variation.

AVERAGE LIFE: 5 to 40 years, depending on maintenance. Machine-sheared hedges do not live as long as hand-pruned plants.

ORIGIN: West Indies and south Florida.

CAUTIONS: None known

SPACING: 18 to 24 inches on center for a hedge. Up to 4 feet on center for a tall mass.

One of our best hedge plants. Makes a good specimen for a native garden as well.

Cocoplum as a hedge

General: Red Tip Cocoplum is one of the best and most common hedges in south Florida. It outperforms the more popular Ficus because it is easier to maintain. It does not grow as fast, which means it requires more patience from the owner while waiting for the plant to grow to the desired size. An all green variety is also available; it is not as colorful but much more tolerant to cold.

Firebush   *Gumbo Limbo*   *Geiger Tree*

Some native companions

Companions: For a native garden, use Cocoplum with Palmettos, Pines, Gumbo Limbos, Silver Buttonwoods, Firebush, and Geiger Trees. For layered hedges, plant Cocoplum between Podocarpus and Dwarf Ilex.

Close-up of Cocoplum leaf with more native companions

Care in the Landscape: Cocoplum is not a heavy feeder but benefits and grows faster with fertilization in March, June, and October of a well-balanced, slow-release mix with minor elements. For an informal look, hand-prune as infrequently as once a year for the first few years. After that, the plant does not require any trimming, if a large specimen is desired. For a hedge, machine shear three or four times per year or as needed to maintain the desired size.

GROWING CONDITIONS

LIGHT: Medium shade to full sun. Prefers full sun but is an acceptable medium shade plant.

WATER: After initial establishment period, low water. Ideal is once a week. Tolerates irrigation up to 3 times a week. Survives without irrigation in average environmental conditions.

SOIL: Wide range

SALT TOLERANCE: Medium. The Red Tip variety is from inland areas and is not as salt tolerant as the green, coastal variety.

WIND TOLERANCE: Medium

ZONE: 10b to 11. The green variety is more cold tolerant than the Red Tip.

PEST PROBLEMS: None known.

PROPAGATION: Cuttings or seeds.

Botanical Name: *Clerodendrum ugandense*

Common Name: **Blue Butterfly**

CHARACTERISTICS

PLANT TYPE: Shrub

AVERAGE SIZE: Easily maintained at sizes between 4 feet tall by 3 feet wide and 6 feet tall by 5 feet wide.

GROWTH RATE: Fast

LEAF: Bright green; about 3 inches long.

FLOWER: Small, about 3/4" wide. Grows in clusters. Resembles blue butterflies.

BEST COLOR: If the winter is unusually warm, it blooms almost continuously.

AVERAGE LIFE: 3 to 8 years.

ORIGIN: Tropical Africa

CAUTIONS: None known

SPACING: 4 feet on center

One of the prettiest and most unique tropical flowers. It resembles a butterfly.

Close-up of the lovely Blue Butterfly flower

General: The Blue Butterfly shrub has lovely flowers. They are small but show well from a distance because of the color contrast between the flowers and the leaves. The shrub is informal, perfect as a background plant in a cottage garden. For people who love flowers, the Blue Butterfly is a must.

Walking Iris   *Angelwing Begonia*   *Blue Daze*

Some companions

Starburst Pentas · Yellow Mussaenda · Ruellia Katie

More companions

Companions: Blue Butterfly looks good with Yellow Mussaenda on either side and a border of Starburst Pentas. If space permits, border the Pentas with mixed colors of Ruellia Katie. Or, try it with Pink Angelwing Begonias on either side and border with Blue Daze. Walking Iris is another great companion for Blue Butterfly.

The Blue Butterfly flowers grow in clusters at the end of the stems.

Care in the Landscape: The Blue Butterfly is easy to grow. Its nutritional needs are low, but it appreciates fertilization in March, June, and October with a well-balanced, slow-release mix with minor elements. Do not make the mistake of trying to keep it shorter than four feet, or you will spend too much time trimming it and lose the flowers. Let it grow large and loose. Trim it once or twice a year when it is not blooming. Remove at least half of every branch with each trimming.

GROWING CONDITIONS

LIGHT: Light shade to full sun. Takes bright sun well and flowers in light but not dense shade.

WATER: After initial establishment period, medium water. Ideal is twice a week. Tolerates irrigation up to 4 times a week. Untested without irrigation.

SOIL: Wide range

SALT TOLERANCE: Low

WIND TOLERANCE: Medium

ZONE: 10b to 11. Cold damage shows by leaf browning, which routinely occurs in the high 30's.

PEST PROBLEMS: None known. I have never seen any bugs or diseases on this plant.

PROPAGATION: Roots easily from cuttings.

Botanical Name: *Codiaeum variegatum 'Petra'*

Common Name: **Petra Croton**

CHARACTERISTICS

PLANT TYPE: Shrub

AVERAGE SIZE: Easily maintained at sizes between 3 feet tall by 2 1/2 feet wide and 6 feet tall by 4 feet wide.

GROWTH RATE: Slow, particularly in the winter. Crotons grow most in summer.

LEAF: Yellow, red, bright pink, green; about 6 inches long.

FLOWER: Insignificant

BEST COLOR: Colorful all year.

AVERAGE LIFE: 15 to 20 years.

ORIGIN: Crotons originated in Malaysia. This one is a hybrid.

CAUTIONS: Milky sap irritates skin and stains clothes. (I have handled Crotons often and never stained my clothes, but be careful.)

SPACING: 2 to 3 feet on center.

Constant color with easy care in sun, shade, salt, or wind.

Before

Left (Before): Shady side yard in need of renovation.

Below (After): Renovation includes layers of shade plants. The large green fern is an Australian Tree Fern. Ti Red Sisters are behind the fern. Petra Crotons are between the Tis, with the Perfection Bromeliads in front. The reds and yellows of the Petras unify the planting.

After

General: The Petra Croton gives bright color with very little care. This Croton is fuller than many other Crotons and is available in three gallon nursery pots with three plants in each pot. Crotons grown this way become much fuller shrubs than those grown with one plant per pot.

Companions: The colors of the Petra Croton contrast well with green tropicals, like palms and the White Bird of Paradise. Accent this Croton with flowering plants that blend with the reds and yellows of the leaves. In sun, try Shrub Allamanda behind Petras with a border of Dwarf Crown of Thorns. Curly Ruffles are also a great background plant for Petras in sun. In shade, plant Firespike behind Petras and border with Wart Ferns. Petra Crotons always look better with a border planted in front.

The Petra Croton viewed from above

Care in the Landscape: Trim as needed to maintain desired size. Crotons of the same type planted in a mass grow at different rates. Keep them trimmed to the same height. If plants look leggy, trim some of the leggy branches back to the ground. If you do this in June or July, as many as three branches sprout from each cut, filling in the bare base. Although Crotons' nutritional needs are low, they benefit and grow faster from fertilization in March, June, and October. Use a well-balanced, slow-release mix that contains minor elements.

Botanical Name: *Codiaeum variegatum 'Red Spot'*

Common Name: **Red Spot Croton**

CHARACTERISTICS

PLANT TYPE: Shrub

AVERAGE SIZE: Easily maintained at sizes between 3 feet tall by 2 1/2 feet wide and 6 feet tall by 4 feet wide.

GROWTH RATE: Medium; little growth in winter. Crotons grow most in summer. This Croton grows faster than most.

LEAF: Yellow, red, bright pink, green; about 6 to 8 inches long by about 1 inch wide.

FLOWER: Insignificant

BEST COLOR: All year

AVERAGE LIFE: 15 to 20 years.

ORIGIN: Crotons originated in Malaysia. This one is a hybrid.

CAUTIONS: Milky sap irritates skin and stains clothes. (I have had no problems, but caution is wise).

SPACING: 2 to 3 feet on center.

Year-round, easy color and an interesting texture with little care.

Red Spot Crotons in front of a Giant Shrimp Plant

General: The Red Spot Croton is a recent addition in many nurseries. It performed very well in our trials. Many Crotons grow tall and leggy but not the Red Spot. It grows full to the ground, producing a great specimen in less time than most other Crotons. Its leaves give an interesting pattern and texture to the garden and works well as an accent or a mass.

Companions: The colors of the Red Spot Croton contrast well with green tropicals, like palms and White Bird of Paradise. Accent this Croton with colorful plants that blend with the reds and yellows of the leaves, like Shrimp Plants and Ti Red Sisters.

Right: Bismarckia Palm underplanted with Ti Red Sisters and Red Spot Crotons. The bright colors of the Tis and Crotons contrast well with the Bismarckia Palm. This combination offers year-round color for many years with very little care.

Below: Close-up of Red Spot Croton.

GROWING CONDITIONS

LIGHT: Medium shade to full sun. Red Spot Crotons take more shade than some other Crotons but not dense shade.

WATER: After initial establishment period, low water. Ideal is once a week. Tolerates irrigation up to 4 times a week. Survives without irrigation in average environmental conditions.

SOIL: Wide range, if well drained.

SALT TOLERANCE: Medium-high.

WIND TOLERANCE: Medium-high

ZONE: 10a to 11. This Croton shows no leaf damage at 37 deg.F.

PEST PROBLEMS: Generally pest free in the landscape; scale, mealybugs and mites are problems occasionally in nurseries.

PROPAGATION: Cuttings or seeds. Cuttings root fastest from May to August.

Care in the Landscape: Trim as needed to maintain desired size. Crotons of the same type planted in a mass grow at different rates. Keep them trimmed to the same height. If plants look leggy, trim some of the leggy branches back to the ground. If you do this in June or July, as many as three branches sprout from each cut, filling in the bare base. Although Crotons' nutritional needs are low, they benefit and grow faster from fertilization in March, June, and October. Use a well-balanced, slow-release mix that contains minor elements.

Botanical Name: *Conocarpus erectus var. sericeus*

Common Name: **Silver Buttonwood Shrub**

CHARACTERISTICS

PLANT TYPE: Shrub or tree. See pages 154 and 155 for information about tree.

AVERAGE SIZE: Easily maintained at sizes between 3 feet tall by 2 feet wide and 20 feet tall by 8 feet wide.

GROWTH RATE: Medium

LEAF: Silver-green; about 2 inches long by 3/4" wide.

FLOWER: Insignificant

BEST COLOR: No seasonal variation.

AVERAGE LIFE: 50 years

ORIGIN: South Florida and the West Indies.

CAUTIONS: None known

SPACING: 18 to 24 inches on center for a hedge; 6 to 8 feet on center for a tree.

An excellent shrub for hedges near the sea. Great companion for bright pinks and purples.

Silver Buttonwood hedge along the ocean. Seagrape is behind the Buttonwood.

General: The Silver Buttonwood is an excellent choice for hedges near the sea. It is native to these areas and thrives in salt air. If planted too far inland, it can experience frequent problems with sooty mold. The silver foliage on this Buttonwood is unique and beautiful. It grows into a tree if unpruned. The Green Buttonwood is a green variety that is commonly available.

Geiger Tree   Gumbo Limbo   Firebush

Some native companions

Companions: For a salt-tolerant garden, plant Silver Buttonwood with Purple Queens, Crown of Thorns, and Crotons. Some appropriate native companions include the Gumbo Limbo Tree, Geiger Tree, and Firebush. For layered hedges, plant Lakeview Jasmine as the back layer, Silver Buttonwood in the middle, and border with Dwarf Ixora.

Silver Buttonwood with some salt-tolerant companions

Care in the Landscape: Silver Buttonwood prefers hand pruning over machine shearing. If continually machine-sheared, it sometimes becomes hollow on the inside. If hand-pruned with deep, judicious cuts, the plant develops a more natural and full form. For a manicured look, hand-prune once a year and machine-shear the rest of the time. Silver Buttonwood is not a heavy feeder but benefits and grows faster if fertilized in March, June, and October with a well-balanced, slow-release mix with minor elements.

GROWING CONDITIONS

LIGHT: Full sun

WATER: After initial establishment period, low water. Ideal is once a week. Tolerates irrigation up to twice a week. Survives without irrigation in average environmental conditions. Do not overwater this plant.

SOIL: Wide range

SALT TOLERANCE: High; performs best close to the sea.

WIND TOLERANCE: High

ZONE: 10b to 11

PEST PROBLEMS: Few problems in its native habitat, near the ocean. Sooty mold, scale, and mites occur inland.

PROPAGATION: Cuttings, seeds.

Botanical Name: *Cordyline terminalis 'Red Sister'*

Common Name: Ti Plant, Red Sister

CHARACTERISTICS

PLANT TYPE: Shrub

AVERAGE SIZE: Easily maintained at sizes between 3 feet tall by 2 feet wide and 5 feet tall by 3 feet wide.

GROWTH RATE: Medium

LEAF: Summer growth is dark burgundy. Winter growth is hot pink, almost red. Leaf measures about 8 inches long by 3 inches wide.

FLOWER: Insignificant

BEST COLOR: All year, but brighter in cooler weather.

AVERAGE LIFE: 10 years

ORIGIN: Eastern Asia

CAUTIONS: None known

SPACING: Plant 3 gallon nursery pots - that each contain 3 or 4 plants - 15 inches on center. This is tighter spacing than most plants. Plant a minimum of 9 stalks (generally 3 pots) in a clump. Tis that are sparsely planted look skimpy. I have used as many as 20 pots in a clump.

Strong color accent with little care if you learn to prune it once a year.

Use Tis in groups of at least nine stems. Smaller groups look skimpy. Be sure to border the bottom stems so that the attractive top leaves show and not the unattractive bottom stems.

General: Ti Red Sister is one of the most colorful plants in the subtropics. The bright pink to fuchsia leaves give year-round color with very little care. The vertical shape of the Ti Plant is very useful in situations where tall, narrow plant shapes are needed, like in-between two windows. In clumps with at least nine stems, Ti Plants will produce dramatic color accents. Most three gallon plants have three stems. The plant is tolerant of low-to-high light, providing it started life in similar conditions. You may avoid Ti Plants because many in Florida look shabby. People are afraid to trim them for fear of killing them. You cannot kill a Ti Plant by trimming it!

Companions: The Ti Red Sister is one of the most useful plants available for color. Its bright pink tones add definition and drama to both tropical landscapes and flower gardens. Some good companions include Crotons, Philodendron Xanadus, Allamandas, and Shrimp Plants. Be sure to border Ti plants with shrubs or groundcovers, like Liriope, Shrimp Plants, or Pentas, to hide the bottom stems. Red Sisters are also very attractive when combined with variegated plants, like Sanchezia or Snowbush.

Before

After

Left, a pool area in need of renovation with plants that will not be constantly dropping debris in the pool. Right, Tis are surrounded by Corkscrew Crotons and bordered by Aztec Grass (Variegated Liriope) and Purple Queen.

Care in the Landscape: Fertilize in March, June, and October with a well-balanced, slow-release mix that contains minor elements. Trimming is the key to its attractiveness in the landscape. Trim once a year in April. Stagger the cuts on the different stalks for a layered effect or trim the tallest one third of the stalks to the ground. Stick the cuttings in soil nearby, and they will root. Some grooming (removing of brown or white leaves) may be needed intermittently throughout the year, especially in early March, to trim off the brown tips and white patches caused by winter cold and wind.

GROWING CONDITIONS

LIGHT: Medium shade to full sun but not dense shade. For a sunny spot, buy a Red Sister that was grown in the sun.

WATER: After initial establishment period, medium water. Ideal is twice a week in sun, once a week in shade. Tolerates wet situations well, as much as 5 irrigations a week. Untested without irrigation.

SOIL: Wide range

SALT TOLERANCE: Low

WIND TOLERANCE: Low

ZONE: 10b to 11. Leaves develop some white patches at 40 deg. F. These white patches, along with some brown tips, are routine in February throughout south Florida. Follow the pruning schedule described on this page. This sensitivity to cold is not problematic enough to prevent the Red Sister's success in south Florida, because the leaf problems last such a short time if the plants are properly pruned in March.

PEST PROBLEMS: Occasional leafspot, scale, or mealybugs. If holes appear in the leaves, it is probably snails. Few pests occur in the landscape.

PROPAGATION: Cuttings. Much easier to root during the spring and summer.

Botanical Name: *Galphimia gracilis*

Common Name: **Thryallis**

CHARACTERISTICS

PLANT TYPE: Shrub

AVERAGE SIZE: Easily maintained at sizes between 4 feet tall by 3 feet wide and 6 feet tall by 4 feet wide.

GROWTH RATE: Medium

LEAF: Light green; 1 to 2 inches long.

FLOWER: Showy yellow, fine-textured flowers in clusters at branch tips.

BEST COLOR: Flowers all year in unusually warm years. Spring through fall in the average year.

AVERAGE LIFE: 10 to 15 years.

ORIGIN: Central and South America.

CAUTIONS: Somewhat brittle. Flops over a bit immediately after planting. It roots well into the ground after it becomes established.

SPACING: 2 to 3 feet on center.

One of the best choices for a large shrub to provide summer color.

Thryallis is the shrub with the yellow flowers. Annual Salvia forms the border.

General: Thryallis is one of your best choices for summer color. When intense heat inhibits blooms on most shrubs, this one is at its peak. Thryallis is very easy to grow and adds a unique, light texture to the garden. Treat it gently while planting because it is somewhat brittle. It also tends to flop, appearing like it is not quite upright, immediately after planting. Do not pile dirt up around the base to straighten it. The plant will anchor itself once it becomes established.

Plumbago   *Walking Iris*   *Starburst Pentas*

Some companions

Thryallis in a country garden

Companions: Use Thryallis as a mass or five-foot rounded specimen. Do not use it among only other greens, as it will appear washed out. Plant it with other flowering plants with blue, pink, orange, or red flowers. Since it is happiest rather tall, use it as a back layer. For the middle layer, plant Plumbago. Border with Starburst or Cranberry Pentas. Blue Porterflower and Firebush are also good companions.

Care in the Landscape: Thryallis is very easy to grow. The most common mistake is to try to maintain it shorter than it wants to be. Thryallis blooms most and is easiest to maintain at four to six feet tall. The second most common mistake is to only trim the tips of the branches and not the whole plant. Trim it <u>hard</u> once a year in winter, after it has stopped flowering. Thryallis recovers well from a hard cutback in winter. This plant is not demanding of fertilizer, but it appreciates feeding in March, June, and October with a well-balanced, slow-release mix that includes minor elements.

Close-up of Thryallis flower

GROWING CONDITIONS

LIGHT: Light shade to full sun. Develops more flowers and a more compact form in sun but produces some flowers in light shade.

WATER: Requires a medium amount of water once it is established, but water heavily for about the first 3 to 6 months after planting. Thryallis sends early thirst signals: it wilts and lower leaves turn yellow. Its heavy need for water abates after it becomes well established in the garden. Ideal water is twice a week in sun or once a week in shade. Untested without irrigation.

SOIL: Wide range, if well drained.

SALT TOLERANCE: Medium

WIND TOLERANCE: Low because it is somewhat brittle.

ZONE: 9 to 11. Survives at least to 28 deg. F.

PEST PROBLEMS: Caterpillars and mites occasionally but relatively pest free.

PROPAGATION: Cuttings and seeds.

Botanical Name: *Graptophyllum pictum*

Common Name: **Caricature Plant or Jamaican Croton**

CHARACTERISTICS

PLANT TYPE: Shrub

AVERAGE SIZE: Easily maintained at sizes between 4 feet tall by 3 feet wide and 7 feet tall by 4 feet wide.

GROWTH RATE: Fast

LEAF: About 3 to 4 inches long by 2 inches wide. Produces a shiny, multicolored pattern that includes bronze and pink. The pattern resembles a caricature. Other colors available are green and yellow and a new one that is green, pink, and yellow.

FLOWER: Purple, about 4 inches long. Beautiful, but occasional. The beauty of this plant is the leaf pattern and color.

BEST COLOR: No seasonal variation.

AVERAGE LIFE: 10 to 20 years.

ORIGIN: New Guinea

CAUTIONS: Cold sensitive for the northern areas of south Florida.

SPACING: 2 to 3 feet on center.

Decorative and easy to grow. Unique bronze and pink colorations.

Caricature Plants are planted under the window to hide a window box. Orchids rest in the window box. Impatiens form the border.

General: The Caricature Plant is unique, decorative, and easy to grow. The bronze and pink color stands out well against light-colored houses. The plant gets its name from the shape of the pattern in the leaves, which resembles a caricature, with no two leaves alike. The Caricature Plant is unusual and deserves more use in south Florida, but it is too cold sensitive for the northern parts of the area. This plant is happy in sun or shade.

Companions: For a monochromatic (one color) look, combine Caricatures with other pink plants, like the Mend Bromeliad, Snowbush, and Angelwing Begonia. For more contrast, consider Sanchezias, Ground Orchids, and Shrimp Plants. Caricatures also look good with green tropicals, like palms and the White Bird of Paradise.

Angelwing Begonia

Mend Bromeliad

Caricature Plant

Snowbush

(Left) Caricature leaves vary in brightness throughout the year. The leaves on the opposite page are quite dark. At times, they are lighter, like the ones above. Some suggested companions are on the right.

Care in the Landscape: Caricature Plants are easy to grow, provided they are allowed to grow at least four feet tall. They can be maintained at this height by trimming about three times a year. To keep them at their minimum three foot height, trim more frequently. Caricature Plants recover quickly from hard cutbacks in the summer. In June, we have cut them as low as 12", and they grew back to a respectable height in a few weeks. Avoid cutting only the tips, or you will produce a leggy plant. Fertilize in March, June, and October with a well-balanced, slow-release mix that contains minor elements.

GROWING CONDITIONS

LIGHT: Medium shade to full sun. Avoid dense shade.

WATER: After initial establishment period, high water in sun or medium water in shade. Ideal is 3 times a week in sun or once or twice a week in shade. Tolerates irrigation up to 5 or 6 times a week.

SOIL: Wide range

SALT TOLERANCE: Low

WIND TOLERANCE: Unknown

ZONE: 10b to 11. Shows cold damage routinely in the northern part of zone 10 in the winter. The leaves turn brown. Recovers when the weather warms up, except in severe freezes.

PEST PROBLEMS: Holes in the leaves usually indicate caterpillars or snails. Occasional scale outbreaks.

PROPAGATION: Cuttings

Botanical Name: *Hamelia patens*

Common Name: **Firebush**

CHARACTERISTICS

PLANT TYPE: Shrub

AVERAGE SIZE: Easily maintained at sizes between 4 feet tall by 4 feet wide and 8 feet tall by 8 feet wide.

GROWTH RATE: Fast

LEAF: Predominately olive green with a red cast at times, particularly during cooler weather. About 3 to 4 inches long.

FLOWER: Orange tubular clusters.

BEST COLOR: Warm months

AVERAGE LIFE: 10 to 20 years.

ORIGIN: Native to Florida and the Caribbean region.

CAUTIONS: None known

SPACING: 3 to 5 feet on center.

A native shrub that blooms most of the year. A favorite of both hummingbirds and butterflies.

Firebush in bloom

General: Use Firebush as a wildlife attractant rather than for showy color. It is not as beautiful as most of the flowering plants in this book, but the wildlife love it; there are few others that attract as many butterflies or hummingbirds. Other wild birds eat the black berries that form after the flowers. Firebush is native to south Florida and works well in the landscape with other natives.

Cocoplum   Gumbo Limbo   Geiger Tree

Some native companions that attract wildlife

Senna suratensis | Blue Porterflower | Starburst Pentas

Some companions to attract butterflies

Companions: Firebush is appropriate for gardens of native Florida plants. A variety of native choices include Cocoplum, Gumbo Limbo, Oak, Silver Buttonwood, and the Geiger Tree. The best companions for a butterfly garden include Pentas, Blue Porterflower, Senna Tree, and Jatropha.

Close-up of Firebush flower

Care in the Landscape: Firebush is easy to grow if allowed to grow naturally, which is large and loose. Plan to spend a lot of time trimming if a small, compact shape is desired. Firebush is not demanding of nutrition, growing naturally in our woods. In a native setting, the leaves falling from trees provide nutrients as they break down around the Firebush's roots; however, in an urban setting, Firebush appreciates a few fertilizations per year.

GROWING CONDITIONS

LIGHT: Light shade to full sun.

WATER: After initial establishment period, low water. Ideal is once a week. Tolerates irrigation up to 3 times a week. Survives without irrigation in average environmental conditions.

SOIL: Wide range

SALT TOLERANCE: Medium

WIND TOLERANCE: Medium

ZONE: 10a to 11. At about 40 deg.F, leaves darken and thin out. Recovers quickly when weather warms up.

PEST PROBLEMS: Grasshoppers.

PROPAGATION: Seeds, cuttings.

Botanical Name: *Ixora 'Nora Grant'*

Common Name: **Ixora Nora Grant**

CHARACTERISTICS

PLANT TYPE: Shrub

AVERAGE SIZE: Easily maintained at sizes between 3 feet tall by 2 feet wide and 10 feet tall by 8 feet wide. Many attempt to maintain it at less than 3 feet with unsatisfactory blooming.

GROWTH RATE: Medium

LEAF: Medium green, glossy; about 2 to 3 inches long.

FLOWER: Coral-pink, about 4 to 5 inches wide.

BEST COLOR: Flowers most in warm months. In an average year, stops flowering from January until March. In an unusually warm year, flowers continuously.

AVERAGE LIFE: 10 to 20 years.

ORIGIN: Asia

CAUTIONS: None known

SPACING: 18 to 36 inches on center. Plant close for a tight, manicured look and further apart for a more natural appearance. 24 inches on center is average.

One of the most popular shrubs in south Florida. Frequently trimmed too often to bloom.

Ixora Nora Grant in full bloom

General: Ixora Nora Grant's large pink flowers and glossy green leaves make it a beautiful shrub. If properly pruned, it is an easy shrub with a long and profuse bloom period. One of the most frequent questions I am asked is why someone's Ixora is not blooming. The most common reason for lack of flowers is poor pruning. Prune Nora Grant heavily in the fall so its branches have time to grow back enough to support flowers in the spring. Constant machine-shearing of this plant causes it to remain permanently green because the branches never get a chance to get long enough to support flowers. And, do not expect profuse flowers in the winter months; Ixora is a warm weather bloomer. Although Nora Grants can be maintained as low as three feet tall, they make excellent large specimen, as shown above.

Companions: An ideal combination includes Pinwheel Jasmine as the back layer, then Snowbush, then Ixora Nora Grant, and a border of Liriope. The Snowbush will outgrow the Pinwheel Jasmine in the beginning. Keep it trimmed lower while the Pinwheel Jasmine catches up.

Ixora Nora Grant and some companions

Care in the Landscape: To promote flowering, trim seldom but deeply. For most blooms, hand-prune hard once a year, just after the plant has stopped blooming in fall. Do not prune so hard that all leaves are removed, because it could kill the plant at this time of the year. If the plant outgrows its space between annual prunings, trim as lightly as possible to maintain desired size. Do not make the common mistake of constantly machine-shearing the tips or the plant will seldom flower. Another common mistake is to attempt to maintain this Ixora at less than three feet tall. It will not flower well if kept this low. Fertilize in March, June, and October with an acidic mix that contains minor elements. Ixoras are heavy feeders and need regular fertilizations.

GROWING CONDITIONS

LIGHT: Light shade to full sun. Flowers more in high light.

WATER: After initial establishment period, medium water. Ideal is twice a week. Tolerates irrigation up to 4 times a week.

SOIL: Prefers slightly acidic soil but performs acceptably in a wide range of soils.

SALT TOLERANCE: Medium

WIND TOLERANCE: Medium

ZONE: 10b to 11. Leaves develop rust-colored spots below 40 deg.F. but recover quickly when it warms up.

PEST PROBLEMS: Relatively problem free in the landscape; aphids and sooty mold occasionally. Not as susceptible to nematodes as some other Ixoras, particularly the Ixora Maui.

PROPAGATION: Cuttings

Botanical Name: *Ixora casei 'Super King'*

Common Name: **Ixora Super King**

CHARACTERISTICS

PLANT TYPE: Shrub

AVERAGE SIZE: Easily maintained at sizes between 2 1/2 feet tall by 2 feet wide and 8 feet tall by 6 feet wide.

GROWTH RATE: Medium

LEAF: Dark green; about 3 inches long.

FLOWER: Red, about 6 inches wide; very showy.

BEST COLOR: Blooms continuously in warm years. In an average year, stops blooming from January until March.

AVERAGE LIFE: 10 to 20 years.

ORIGIN: Southern Asia

CAUTIONS: None known

SPACING: 2 feet on center for a tight look. 3 to 4 feet on center for a taller, more natural look.

One of the showiest Ixoras. The flowers are larger and brighter than the more common Nora Grant.

A recently planted Super King Ixora. This one has a higher percentage of color than most.

General: Ixora Super King is an exceptional shrub with very showy, bright-red flowers that bloom most of the year. The flowers are larger than most, measuring a full six inches across. It is more colorful than the similar Nora Grant. An additional benefit of the Super King is that it can be trimmed smaller than most shrubs and still produce flowers. Super King is an older, little-used plant that deserves more attention.

Podocarpus   *Silver Buttonwood*   *Foxtail Fern*

Some companions

Companions: For a manicured hedge look, plant Podocarpus as the back layer, Silver Buttonwood in the middle, and Ixora Super King in front. For lots of color, plant Shrub Allamanda as back layer, Ixora Super King in the middle, Fire Croton next, and Ruellia Katie as a border. Mixing the Super King with Philodendron Xanadu and Foxtail Fern provides interesting textural contrast.

Close-up of Super King flower with some companions

Care in the Landscape: To promote flowering, trim seldom but deeply. Frequent pruning of the tips of the plant prevents flowering. For most blooms, prune hard once a year, just after the plant has stopped blooming in fall. Do not prune so hard that all leaves are removed because it could kill the plant at this time of the year. If the plant outgrows its space between annual prunings, trim as lightly as possible to maintain desired size. Fertilize in March, June, and October with an acidic fertilizer that contains minor elements. These fertilizations are important to insure the health of the Ixora.

GROWING CONDITIONS

LIGHT: Light shade to full sun; blooms more profusely in bright sun but does reasonably well in partial shade.

WATER: After initial establishment period, medium water. Ideal is twice a week. Tolerates irrigation up to 4 times a week.

SOIL: Prefers slightly acidic soil but performs acceptably in a wide range of soils, if well drained.

SALT TOLERANCE: Medium

WIND TOLERANCE: Medium

ZONE: 10b to 11. More cold sensitive than Ixora Nora Grant.

PEST PROBLEMS: None serious. I have never seen nematodes attack this plant but have heard of it. Some of the older varieties of Ixora are much more susceptible to nematodes.

PROPAGATION: Cuttings

Botanical Name: *Jatropha integerrima 'Compacta'*

Common Name: **Dwarf Jatropha**

One of the few shrubs that blooms all the time. The favorite food of the Zebra butterfly. Very easy to grow.

Jatropha shrub in full bloom

General: Jatropha is one of the few shrubs available that blooms all the time with very little care. It is grown commercially as a shrub or a small tree; however, it grows better as a small tree than as a shrub because of its tendency towards lankiness. Nonetheless, it is useful as a shrub as well, particularly in a butterfly garden if the tree would be too tall. It is not as dramatic as some of the other shrubs with red flowers, notably Firespike, but it blooms more often than any other red shrub. Be sure to specify the 'Compacta' variety when buying Jatropha. As the name implies, it is much more compact than the other, older varieties. Also, be sure to place Jatropha in areas where it can be maintained at least at four feet tall.

Some companions

Companions: Use Jatropha as a mass or shrub specimen. It works well as a mid-to-back layer so that its bareness at the base is hidden. For a very easy combination, use with the three plants shown above in the order shown, with Jatropha the tallest. For a butterfly garden, use Jatropha with Blue Porterflower and Pentas.

LIGHT: Light shade to full sun. Blooms best in full sun.

WATER: After initial establishment period, low water. Ideal is once a week. Tolerates irrigation up to 4 times a week. Untested without irrigation.

SOIL: Wide range

SALT TOLERANCE: Medium

WIND TOLERANCE: Medium

ZONE: 10b to 11

PEST PROBLEMS: Scale or leaf miners occasionally; otherwise, relatively pest free.

PROPAGATION: Cuttings

Close-up of the Jatropha flower

Care in the Landscape: Jatropha is not demanding of fertilizer but appreciates an application in March, June, and October with a well-balanced, slow-release mix with minor elements. Trim once or twice a year, especially in fall or early winter, when the blooming slows down a bit. Trim back rather hard to encourage fullness. Do not attempt to make Jatropha full to the base. This is not its natural growth habit. Plant other layers around the base to hide the bottom branches instead of trying to fight nature.

Botanical Name: *Murraya paniculata 'Lakeview'*

Common Name: **Orange Jasmine, Lakeview Jasmine**

One of south Florida's best hedge plants. Frequently overlooked is its potential for producing a wonderful scent.

Most people are unaware of the fact that Lakeview Jasmine makes a wonderful tall hedge because it is generally thought of as a smaller material. This Jasmine hedge is seven feet tall and requires less trimming than the more commonly used Ficus.

General: Orange Jasmine is most often used as a hedge. Lakeview is an improved variety with slightly larger leaves and flowers. Lakeview Jasmine is an excellent hedge material because of its density and compactness. It is far superior to the more commonly used Ficus as a hedge because of its slower growth rate and greater resistance to cold damage. Its wonderful scent is seldom noticeable when it is trimmed as a hedge, however, because the flowers that create the scent are trimmed off. Lakeview Jasmine is a nice addition to a perennial garden as an informal flowering shrub. It is also grown commercially as a small tree.

Some companions for a manicured look

Companions: Lakeview Jasmine works well as an unstructured shrub in a cottage garden. Since it shears well into a hedge, it is also ideal for a manicured landscape. It mixes well with the plants shown above in a four layered, manicured garden. Use Lakeview Jasmine as the back layer, then Variegated Arboricola, then Dwarf Ixora. Use Juniper as a border.

Close-up of Lakeview Jasmine flower. The actual flower is quite a bit smaller than this photo.

Care in the Landscape: Lakeview Jasmine frequently shows nutritional deficiencies (overall yellowing of the leaves) in poor soils. Fertilize in March, June, and October with a well-balanced, slow-release mix that contains minor elements. For a natural look as a shrub, hard prune twice a year after flowering. For a hedge, shear as needed.

GROWING CONDITIONS

LIGHT: Light shade to full sun.

WATER: After initial establishment period, low water. Ideal is once a week. Tolerates irrigation up to 4 times a week. Untested without irrigation.

SOIL: Wide range

SALT TOLERANCE: Medium

WIND TOLERANCE: Medium

ZONE: 9 to 11. Dies back at 30 deg. F. but recovers with warm weather.

PEST PROBLEMS: Infrequent in the landscape. Occasional whiteflies, sooty mold and scale.

PROPAGATION: Cuttings and seeds.

Botanical Name: *Mussaenda philippinensis*

Common Name: **Yellow or Dwarf Mussaenda**

CHARACTERISTICS

PLANT TYPE: Shrub

AVERAGE SIZE: Easily maintained at sizes between 4 feet tall by 3 feet wide and 6 feet tall by 4 feet wide.

GROWTH RATE: Medium

LEAF: Medium green; about 1 inch long.

FLOWER: White bract, about 1 inch long, with small yellow flower.

BEST COLOR: On the average, blooms from April to December. Blooms all year in warm areas. Stops blooming at about 45 deg. F. Shows cold damage in high 30 deg. F.

AVERAGE LIFE: 10 to 15 years

ORIGIN: Unknown

CAUTIONS: Looks poorly in the winter in the northern parts of south Florida or all over south Florida in an unusually cold year. Recovers quickly in spring.

SPACING: 3 feet on center

A little-known plant with a long blooming season and beautiful flowers. Deserves much more use in south Florida.

Yellow Mussaenda in full bloom. It shows well up close or from a distance and has a high percentage of color.

General: Yellow Mussaenda is a fabulous plant. Offering a high percentage of color for much of the year, it is not demanding of care. The unique bloom is two colors, yellow and white. Technically, the yellow part is the flower and the white part is the bract. The effect is lovely, showing well up close or at a distance. Take care in placing this shrub because of the potential for winter cold damage on the leaves. Avoid planting Yellow Mussaenda in locations where it would be a key focal point in winter.

Firespike Blue Porterflower Shrimp Ground Orchids

Some companions

Companions: Yellow Mussaenda looks good with most other plants. In sun, try Plumbago in front of Mussaenda and border the Plumbago with Starburst Pentas. In sun or shade, plant Yellow Mussaendas around Firespikes, bordering the mass with Mammey Crotons. Pink Angelwing Begonias and Blue Butterflies make excellent companions in shade. Blue Porterflowers, Shrimps, and Ground Orchids are also good companions in sun or shade.

Close-up of the Yellow Mussaenda flower

Care in the Landscape: Fertilize Yellow Mussaenda in March, June, and October with a well-balanced, slow-release mix that includes minor elements. Trim *hard* once a year after the shrub has stopped blooming, generally in winter or early spring. Trim back quite short at this time - to about two feet tall. If the weather is still cool, do not cut so short you remove all the leaves, but cut more than just the tips. The shrub will not look full during summer if only the tips are trimmed. Trim again if the shrub grows taller than desired in summer. The second trimming can be minor.

GROWING CONDITIONS

LIGHT: Medium shade to full sun. This is an excellent choice for shade color. Avoid dense shade.

WATER: After initial establishment period, medium water. Ideal is twice a week in sun or once a week in shade. Tolerates irrigation up to 6 times a week. Untested without irrigation.

SOIL: Wide range

SALT TOLERANCE: Unknown

WIND TOLERANCE: Unknown

ZONE: 10b to 11. Shows cold damage in high 30's . The leaves thin out and darken. It does not completely defoliate like some other Mussaendas.

PEST PROBLEMS: None known in the landscape. I saw scale once in a nursery.

PROPAGATION: Cuttings; propagate only in summer.

Botanical Name: *Odontonema strictum*

Common Name: **Firespike**

CHARACTERISTICS

PLANT TYPE: Shrub

AVERAGE SIZE: Easily maintained at sizes between 4 feet tall by 3 feet wide and 6 feet tall by 5 feet wide.

GROWTH RATE: Fast

LEAF: Dark green and pointed; 3 to 4 inches long.

FLOWER: Red spikes ranging from 4 to 8 inches long. Dramatic and showy.

BEST COLOR: In an average year, blooms from June until February. Blooms all year if winter is unusually warm, but stops flowering in most years when temperatures drop into the 40's.

AVERAGE LIFE: 10 to 20 years.

ORIGIN: Tropical America

CAUTIONS: None known

SPACING: 3 to 5 feet on center.

Dramatic red flower spikes attract butterflies and are the favorite food of hummingbirds.

Firespike in full bloom

General: Firespike is a fabulous plant. It gives at least six months of color each year with minimal care. Firespike was chosen as 'Plant of the Year' in 1998 by the Florida Nurserymen and Growers Association. Its spectacular color should be part of every garden. I have a pair of hummingbirds that come to my garden to live every winter. Although the hummingbirds love the nectar from many flowers, they spend the most time on the Firespike. Hummingbirds are currently rare in south Florida. Maybe if every person who reads this book plants a Firespike in their garden, the hummingbirds will return.

Companions: For an easy summer garden, plant Ruellia Purple Showers on either side of Firespike. Use Yellow Mussaenda as the next layer and border with Starburst Pentas. In shade, Firespike is a good companion for the Angelwing Begonias and Crotons.

Ruellia Purple Showers

Yellow Mussaenda

Firespike

Starburst Pentas

Close-up of Firespike flower with some companions

Care in the Landscape: Firespike is very easy to grow. It is not demanding of food but appreciates fertilization in March, June, and October with a well-balanced, slow-release mix that contains minor elements. The key to its success is a yearly, hard cutback. Cut it almost to the ground when it stops flowering, generally in February. Do not cut it back hard again until the following year at the same time. You can groom it in-between the hard cutbacks. Occasionally, a branch will fall on the ground. Cut that one back to the base at any time.

GROWING CONDITIONS

LIGHT: Medium shade to full sun. Blooms the same in either situation. Not for dense shade.

WATER: After initial establishment period, low. Ideal is once a week. Tolerates irrigation up to 6 times a week. Untested without irrigation.

SOIL: Wide range

SALT TOLERANCE: Low

WIND TOLERANCE: Low

ZONE: 7 to 11. The plant dies back after a freeze but recovers.

PEST PROBLEMS: Snails occasionally.

PROPAGATION: Cuttings. Very easy to root.

Botanical Name: *Pachystachys lutea*

Common Name: **Shrimp Plant, Golden Shrimp Plant**

CHARACTERISTICS

PLANT TYPE: Shrub

AVERAGE SIZE: Easily maintained at sizes between 3 feet tall by 2 feet wide and 6 feet tall by 3 feet wide.

GROWTH RATE: Medium

LEAF: Green and pointed; 2 to 3 inches long.

FLOWER: Dramatic yellow spike with white accent; about 3 inches long.

BEST COLOR: One of the few plants that blooms every day of the year.

AVERAGE LIFE: 5 years

ORIGIN: Mexico

CAUTIONS: None

SPACING: 18 to 24 inches on center.

One of the best plants in this book. Dramatic, beautiful flowers every day of the year with very little care in sun or shade.

For a tropical look, use Shrimps with Tis and Mammey Crotons.

General: The Shrimp Plant is the favorite of most people who visit our trial gardens. The flower is very showy and quite unique, a yellow spike with an accent of white. It is one of the few plants that flowers all year, even during our coolest or our hottest days. The Shrimp gives much more color impact than most other perennials, in either sun or shade. Hide its tendency to legginess with smaller shrubs or groundcovers as a lower layer.

Angelwing Begonias   *Yellow Mussaenda*   *Blue Daze*

Some companions

Companions: The Shrimp Plant is very versatile, combining well with most other plants. For an easy sun garden, plant Shrimp as the tallest layer, Cranberry Pentas as the middle layer, and Ruellia Katie as a front border. In shade, Shrimp is beautiful in front of Angelwing Begonias.

Shrimp Plant with more companions

Care in the Landscape: Fertilize Shrimp Plants in March, June, and October with a well-balanced, slow-release mix that contains minor elements. Shrimps are heavy feeders. The minor elements are especially important. If all the leaves yellow slightly, fertilize again. Hand pruning is essential for the success of this plant. One method is to cut back drastically (to short sticks) in the summer. It takes about six weeks to recover. Another pruning method is stagger-cutting. Cut about one third of the plant back at a time, cutting the tallest branches to the ground. This method keeps constant new shoots growing at the base of the plant. Stagger-cutting is generally done about twice a year and produces constant blooms. If the Shrimp Plant is cut from September through February, the stalks that are cut will not bloom until the following summer.

GROWING CONDITIONS

LIGHT: Light to medium shade is ideal. Tolerates full sun but prefers some break from the intense light. I have used it hundreds of times in full sun. Considering the positive attributes of this plant, it outperforms any other yellow I have seen, even in full sun.

WATER: After initial establishment, low. Ideal is twice a week in sun or once a week in shade. Tolerates irrigation up to 3 times a week. Does not do well with too much water. Untested without irrigation.

SOIL: Wide range

SALT TOLERANCE: Medium

WIND TOLERANCE: Low

ZONE: 9 to 11. At 32 deg. F, growth above ground dies back. Plant generally grows back as long as it is not further north than zone 9.

PEST PROBLEMS: Few pest problems after it is well established in the ground. Caterpillars or snails occasionally eat holes in the leaves if the plant is in a pot or recently planted in the ground.

PROPAGATION: Easily propagated by cuttings at any time of the year.

Botanical Name: *Pentas lanceolata 'Cranberry'*

Common Name: **Cranberry Pentas**

CHARACTERISTICS

PLANT TYPE: Shrub

AVERAGE SIZE: Easily maintained at sizes between 2 feet tall by 1 1/2 feet wide and 4 feet tall by 2 feet wide.

GROWTH RATE: Fast

LEAF: Medium green and pointed; about 2 inches long.

FLOWER: Bright pink, almost red clusters; about 2 to 3 inches wide.

BEST COLOR: All year

AVERAGE LIFE: 1 to 3 years

ORIGIN: Tropical Africa

CAUTIONS: Short-lived (but inexpensive).

SPACING: 18 inches on center for a tight look; 24 inches for a more natural appearance.

One of the most intense flower colors in this book. Easy to grow and inexpensive. Great butterfly plant. Best of 16 different Pentas in field trials.

Cranberry Pentas are in the center of this garden. Purple Pentas are in the top of the picture. Yellow Lantana borders the pool screening. A few blue Plumbago flowers show in front.

General: A welcome addition (1995) to the myriad of Pentas, Cranberry is the first medium-sized Penta to produce intensely colored blooms. The old Red Pentas are larger. The New Look series of dwarf Pentas are almost as intense but much shorter-lived and smaller. The New Look Pentas have white flower centers, while the Cranberry is solid hot pink. The New Look Pentas do not give anywhere near the color intensity as the Cranberry, especially from a distance. The low price and spectacular color of the Cranberry make it extremely worthwhile in the landscape. These Pentas are one of the best plants for butterfly gardens.

Companions: For easy, bright color, plant Shrimp Plants behind Cranberry Pentas. Border with Ruellia Katies. To attract butterflies, plant Cranberry Pentas in back, Blue Porterflower in the middle, and border with Yellow Lantana. Cranberry Pentas are a wonderful border for Snowbush. Another winning combination: plant Thryallis and Firespike behind Cranberry Pentas, with Plumbago in front.

Cranberry Pentas with some companions

Care in the Landscape: For a wild look, cut back hard (to sticks) once a summer. Since Pentas have a tendency to get fungus, they benefit from this hard summer cutback. The thinning of the plant allows air to circulate, thus inhibiting fungus. For a more compact look, trim often, even monthly in the summer. Cranberry Pentas can be machine-sheared into a boxlike hedge, but frequent trimming inhibits flowering. Fertilize this plant in March, June, and October with a well-balanced, slow-release mix that contains minor elements.

Botanical Name: *Philodendron 'Xanadu'*

Common Name: **Philodendron Xanadu**

CHARACTERISTICS

PLANT TYPE: Shrub

AVERAGE SIZE: 3 to 4 feet tall by 3 to 4 feet wide. This plant cannot be maintained any smaller.

GROWTH RATE: Medium

LEAF: Dark, glossy green; becomes larger as the plant grows.

FLOWER: Inconspicuous

BEST COLOR: No seasonal variation.

AVERAGE LIFE: 5 to 15 years.

ORIGIN: Hybrid

CAUTIONS: Sap is an irritant.

SPACING: 3 to 4 feet on center. Most Xanadus are planted too close.

Tropical texture with little care. Good as a mass or accent. Compact substitute for the larger Philodendron selloum.

The Xanadu is the plant to the far right. It fits in well with a manicured look, as shown with Dwarf Crown of Thorns and Roebeleniis.

General: The Philodendron Xanadu is one of the few plants available that gives a tropical texture in sun or shade without growing very large. It is a good substitute for the larger Philodendron selloum when seeking a more compact look. Versatile in style, it adapts to manicured, tropical, or even cottage gardens. Avoid the common mistake of underestimating the mature size of this plant. When I used it for the first time, I placed it in front of Petra Crotons, thinking that the Crotons could be maintained at three feet and the Xanadus at two feet. A year later, the Xanadus were a foot taller than the Crotons behind them! Xanadus cannot be maintained smaller than three to four feet tall and three to four feet wide. Also, avoid planting Xanadus in areas that are wet and expect to lose about five per cent in the best situations.

Companions: Use Xanadus as specimen or masses. Three together, planted in a triangle, make a nice accent for the center of a bed of lower plants. For a manicured look, pair this Philodendron with palms, Foxtail Ferns, Variegated Arboricolas, and Dwarf Crown of Thorns. For a tropical look, mix with Crotons, Cardboard Palms, and Ti plants.

Philodendron Xanadu

Variegated Arboricola *Dwarf Crown of Thorns* *Foxtail Fern*

Philodendron Xanadu with some companions

Care in the Landscape: Trim occasionally to remove dead leaves. Xanadus cannot be reduced in height by trimming. Fertilize in March, June, and October with a well-balanced, slow-release mix with minor elements.

LIGHT: Medium shade to full sun. Not dense shade.

WATER: After initial establishment period, low water. Ideal is once a week in shade, twice a week in sun or wind. Overwatering causes fungus, which is the most common problem with this plant. Untested without irrigation.

SOIL: Wide range, if well drained. Xanadus do poorly in wet soil.

SALT TOLERANCE: Medium

WIND TOLERANCE: Medium

ZONE: 10a to 11

PEST PROBLEMS: A leaf spot fungus (that looks like brown patches) frequently appears soon after planting. It usually disappears after the plant gets established, about 6 months in the ground.

PROPAGATION: Tissue culture.

Botanical Name: *Plumbago auriculata*

Common Name: **Plumbago**

An extraordinary performer that blooms most of the year with very little care. The blue color is unique and beautiful.

Plumbago is the blue shrub in front. Thryallis is the yellow shrub in back.

General: Plumbago offers the advantages of a long flowering period with easy care. Its unique blue color adds the contrast that makes garden colors really show. Alone, Plumbago is not particularly impressive, but comes to life when contrasted with pinks and yellows. Its light texture fits in well with the cottage garden look. It does not hedge well and does not fit in a manicured landscape. Plumbago is a very informal plant with the casual style of a wildflower.

Note: The new brighter blue Plumbago cultivars have been available since the early 1990's. They are far superior to the old, washed out blues. The newer cultivars also bloom more and are easier to maintain.

Companions: A beautiful cottage garden idea is to plant Thryallis on either side of an Anderson Crepe Hibiscus tree. Plant Plumbago behind and in front of the same tree. Plumbago is also a wonderful companion for Cranberry Pentas, Shrimp Plants, Yellow Mussaendas, and Shrub Ruellias.

Plumbago will climb an arch if planted next to it. It is easier to control than most south Florida vines.

Close-up of Plumbago flower

Care in the Landscape: Do not attempt to trim Plumbago into a hedge. It is very informal and will not adapt to a disciplined look. Simply trim as needed to preserve the size you want. Unlike many of the plants in this book, Plumbago does not need a hard annual cutback. We let ours get quite tall, trimming it hard only every two years. Trim it in winter, when it has stopped blooming. Fertilize in March, June, and October with a well-balanced, slow-release mix that contains minor elements.

GROWING CONDITIONS

LIGHT: Light shade to full sun. Flowers best in full sun.

WATER: After initial establishment period, low water. Ideal is once a week, or twice a week in a windy location. Overwatering causes fungus, which is the most common problem with this plant. Untested without irrigation.

SOIL: Wide range

SALT TOLERANCE: Medium

WIND TOLERANCE: Medium

ZONE: 10a to 11. Tolerates 25 deg. F.

PEST PROBLEMS: None serious; scale or mites occasionally. Develops fungus if kept too wet. If the plant has fungus, parts of it turn black, become slimy, and die back. Cut back on water if fungus develops. Spray with a fungicide if it becomes severe.

PROPAGATION: Cuttings

TIP FOR ECONOMY: Plumbago covers a large area for a small price if purchased in 1 gallon containers and planted 3 feet on center.

Botanical Name: *Podocarpus macrophyllus*

Common Name: **Podocarpus**

CHARACTERISTICS

PLANT TYPE: Shrub or tree

AVERAGE SIZE: Easily maintained at sizes between 30 inches tall by 16 inches wide and 35 feet tall by 10 feet wide. Most commonly used as a hedge in the 6 foot range.

GROWTH RATE: Medium

LEAF: Dark green; needlelike, about 1 to 2 inches long.

FLOWER: Insignificant

BEST COLOR: No seasonal change.

AVERAGE LIFE: At least 30 years.

ORIGIN: Japan

CAUTIONS: Drops leaves heavily so plant away from pavement.

SPACING: For a hedge, 18 to 24 inches on center.

An excellent shrub for hedges or manicured specimens.

Podocarpus as a manicured specimen

General: Like most hedge plants, Podocarpus grows into a tree if not trimmed. It is primarily used as a hedge or clipped specimen because its dense form is ideal for trimming. Podocarpus hedges are very attractive and easy to maintain but slow to mature. If planted in the most common three gallon pot size, they appear quite thin for six to twelve months after planting. Larger specimens, in at least seven gallon pots, are much faster to fill in. Many prefer the faster growing Ficus initially, until the Ficus is growing so rapidly that it requires almost weekly pruning in the summer to maintain its manicured form. Podocarpus hedges only require trimming a few times each year. The evergreen texture of Podocarpus is an interesting mix with larger leaf plants, like Cocoplum or Viburnum.

Companions: Podocarpus works well in an arrangement of layered hedges. Use it as the back layer, with Super King Ixora in the middle and a border of Viburnum. It also mixes well with Silver Buttonwood, Lakeview Jasmine, and Cocoplum.

Close-up of Podocarpus leaves

Podocarpus is used to break up the space between windows.

Care in the Landscape: Podocarpus is not a heavy feeder but benefits and grows faster if fertilized in March, June, and October with a well-balanced, slow-release mix with minor elements. Trim as needed. Machine shearing is ideal.

GROWING CONDITIONS

LIGHT: Light shade to full sun.

WATER: After initial establishment period, medium water. Ideal is once or twice a week. Tolerates irrigation up to 3 or 4 times a week. Untested without irrigation.

SOIL: Wide range

SALT TOLERANCE: Medium

WIND TOLERANCE: Medium

ZONE: 7 to 11

PEST PROBLEMS: Scale and sooty mold.

PROPAGATION: Seeds, cuttings.

Botanical Name: *Ruellia brittoniana 'Purple Showers'*

Common Name: Ruellia Purple Showers, Mexican Bluebell

CHARACTERISTICS

PLANT TYPE: Shrub (See page 46 and 47 for Ruellia Katie, a smaller Ruellia).

AVERAGE SIZE: Easily maintained at sizes between 3 feet tall by 2 feet wide and 5 feet tall by 3 feet wide.

GROWTH RATE: Fast

LEAF: Dark green, thin, pointed; about 3 inches long by 3/4 inch wide.

FLOWER: Purple; bell-shaped, about 1 inch wide.

BEST COLOR: Warm months

AVERAGE LIFE: 10 years

ORIGIN: Mexico

CAUTIONS: Sends up sprouts that can be a nuisance but not as bad as the pink variety.

SPACING: 2 feet on center

Outstanding shrub that gives great color for much of the year with very little care.

Ruellia growing with Shrimp Plants

General: Ruellia Purple Showers is a gardener's dream - lots of color with very little effort. I was hesitant to use it when I first saw it because of Ruellia's reputation of uncontrollable spreading. However, my extensive Ruellia field trials have shown it to be quite manageable. The pink shrub variety is much more invasive and does not flower anywhere near as much. This shrub Ruellia is attractive when used with other colors, especially with reds or hot pinks and yellows. Its color fades when used with other greens. Ruellia Purple Showers' ability to flower in light shade is an additional benefit.

Angelwing Begonia   *Ruellia Purple Showers*   *Walking Iris*

Angelwing Begonia and Walking Iris are excellent companions for Ruellia in light shade.

Companions: Use Ruellia Purple Showers in informal gardens. It works well with other informal flowering plants. Shrubs that work well behind this Ruellia include Curly Ruffle, Shrub Allamanda, Angelwing Begonia, Thryallis, Jatropha, and Firespike. The Ruellia will attempt to outgrow these back layers in the beginning. Trim to keep it lower than the back layers. In time, the back plantings will outgrow the Ruellia. Shrubs or groundcovers that work well in front of Ruellia include Shrimp Plants, Cranberry Pentas, Dwarf Powderpuffs, Walking Irises, and Dwarf Chenilles. Yellow Mussaenda works well behind or in front of Ruellia.

Allamanda

Ruellia Purple Showers

Cranberry Pentas

Allamanda and Cranberry Pentas are excellent companions for Ruellia in sun or light shade.

Care in the Landscape: Ruellia Purple Showers is not demanding of care. It grows very quickly immediately after planting. If it outgrows the layers behind it, trim it aggressively until the back layers have a chance to catch up. After establishment (about six months in the ground), its growth rate slows down. From that point forward, trim it to maintain the desired size. This shrub recovers well from hard cutbacks in the summer, flowering again quickly. Not demanding of fertilizer, it benefits from a feeding in March, June and October with a well-balanced, slow-release mix that contains minor elements.

GROWING CONDITIONS

LIGHT: Light shade to full sun. Blooms acceptably in a light shade situation and takes direct sun beautifully.

WATER: After initial establishment, medium. Ideal is once a week in shade or twice a week in sun or wind. Tolerates irrigation up to 5 or 6 times a week. Untested without irrigation.

SOIL: Wide range

SALT TOLERANCE: Medium

WIND TOLERANCE: Medium

ZONE: 10a to 11

PEST PROBLEMS: None known.

PROPAGATION: Cuttings, seeds.

NOTE: There are many different types of Ruellia. The shrub Ruellias are available in three colors: white, pink, or purple. I have tried the purple and pink, with the purple far outperforming the pink. I have not yet extensively tried the white. The groundcover Ruellias are covered on pages 46 and 47.

Botanical Name: *Sanchezia speciosa*

Common Name: **Sanchezia**

CHARACTERISTICS

PLANT TYPE: Shrub

AVERAGE SIZE: Easily maintained at sizes between 3 feet tall by 3 feet wide and 7 feet tall by 5 feet wide.

GROWTH RATE: Medium

LEAF: Medium green with yellow stripes; about 4 inches long.

FLOWER: Yellow to orange on a long spike. Although the flower is very interesting, its appearance is occasional. Use Sanchezia for the beauty of its foliage.

BEST COLOR: Flowers add color occasionally in spring, summer, and fall. But foliage adds color at all times.

AVERAGE LIFE: 10 to 20 years.

ORIGIN: Ecuador

CAUTIONS: Cold sensitive in the northern parts of south Florida and in all of south Florida in unusually cold winters.

SPACING: 2 feet on center for a tight look; 3 to 4 feet, for a more loose, natural appearance.

Tropical texture and unique striped leaves fit into any garden style. Good companion for plants with dark leaves.

Sanchezia bordered with Dwarf Chenille. Ti Red Sisters appear in the upper left. Bromeliads flower behind.

General: Sanchezia is a very tropical looking shrub that thrives in sun or shade. It is not particularly notable alone but comes alive when complemented with other plants. It is quite cold sensitive in the northern parts of south Florida.

Curly Raffle   Ti Red Sister   Philodendron Xanadu

Some companions

Companions: The variegated foliage of Sanchezia glows when mixed with either green, tropical textures or bright colors. Coarse textures that compliment Sanchezia include palms, Curly Ruffle, White Bird of Paradise, Philodendron Xanadu and Wart Fern. Bright colors that contrast well with Sanchezia include Ti Plants, Crotons, Super King Ixoras, Dwarf Crown of Thorns, Firespikes, and Dwarf Chenilles.

Sanchezia

Mammey Croton *Wart Fern* *Dwarf Crown of Thorns*

Close-up of Sanchezia leaves with other companions

Care in the Landscape: Sanchezia is a very easy plant. Fertilize in March, June, and October with a well-balanced, slow-release mix that contains minor elements. Trim as needed to maintain size. Sanchezia is a naturally full plant and easy to keep well groomed. If leaves brown during the winter months, it is probably cold damage. If possible, wait until March to trim because trimming too hard in winter could cause it to die in a freeze.

GROWING CONDITIONS

LIGHT: Medium shade to full sun. Not dense shade.

WATER: After initial establishment period, high water in sun and medium in shade. Ideal is twice a week in sun or once or twice a week in shade. Tolerates irrigation up to 6 times a week.

SOIL: Wide range

SALT TOLERANCE: Medium

WIND TOLERANCE: Medium

ZONE: 10b to 11. If browning of the leaves occurs in winter, it is cold damage. Leaf tips will burn at about 38 deg. F., which routinely occurs in zone 10b. I still recommend it for this zone, however, because it recovers quickly. Trim off the brown leaves in March. Do not use it in zone 10a or further north.

PEST PROBLEMS: If holes appear in the leaves, they are caused by snails or caterpillars. They feed at night and are not frequently visible in the daytime. Treat with snail bait or spray for caterpillars if damage is severe. I have never seen any other pests in the landscape but have heard of occasional attacks from mealybugs.

PROPAGATION: Cuttings

Botanical Name: *Schefflera arboricola 'Trinette'*

Common Name: **Variegated Arboricola Trinette**

CHARACTERISTICS

PLANT TYPE: Shrub

AVERAGE SIZE: Easily maintained at sizes between 2 feet tall by 2 feet wide and 8 feet tall by 4 feet wide. Because of its slow growth rate, it is usually maintained at smaller sizes.

GROWTH RATE: Slow. Slower than the common green variety.

LEAF: Dark green and light yellow; about 1 1/2 inches long.

FLOWER: Insignificant

BEST COLOR: No seasonal variation.

AVERAGE LIFE: 20 years or more.

ORIGIN: Hybrid. Originally from Taiwan.

CAUTIONS: None known

SPACING: 2 feet on center

An attractive, durable plant that handles wind, sun, salt, or shade while requiring little care.

Variegated Arboricolas are the plants with the yellow and green leaves. They surround Shrimp Plants and Ti Red Sisters.

General: Green Arboricola has been used for many years in south Florida. The newer, variegated forms are a great improvement, not only because they are more attractive, but also because they are slower growing and easier to control. Trinette is the most colorful of the variegated forms. It is a great choice for difficult environments, like wind, salt, bright sun, or dense shade. Trinette handles deep shade better than most colorful plants.

Companions: For an easy garden in sun or shade, use Arboricolas as a border for Ti Plants and Shrimps, as shown opposite. Another easy grouping, especially valuable in moderate salt environments, combines Trinettes with Fire Crotons, bordered with Dwarf Crown of Thorns. In dense shade, combine Trinettes with Walking Irises and ferns.

Variegated Arboricola Trinette

Mammey Croton   Dwarf Crown of Thorns

Variegated Arboricola Trinette with some companions

Care in the Landscape: Trinettes are very easy to grow. Fertilize in March, June, and October with a well-balanced, slow-release mix that contains minor elements. Trim as needed to control height. Trinettes grow to the ground and do not require special pruning. If grown in full sun and heavily pruned in summer, the interior of the plant can temporarily burn from the sun. This is due to the plant being unaccustomed to that amount of sun in the past. There is less chance of burning if trimmed in the cooler months.

Botanical Name: *Stachytarpheta urticifolia*

Common Name: **Blue Porterflower, Blue Porterweed**

CHARACTERISTICS

PLANT TYPE: Shrub

AVERAGE SIZE: Easily maintained at sizes between 3 feet tall by 2 feet wide and 4 feet tall by 4 feet wide.

GROWTH RATE: Fast

LEAF: Medium green, looks like mint; about 1 inch long.

FLOWER: Unusual spikes of green hold blue flowers; the blue portion is about 1/2 inch long.

BEST COLOR: Blooms most of the year, stopping in the cool months.

AVERAGE LIFE: 5 years

ORIGIN: Tropical America, but not Florida. Another Porterflower, a groundcover, is native to Florida.

CAUTIONS: Reseeds some but not enough to become a nuisance.

SPACING: 2 feet on center for a tight look; 3 feet on center for a natural look.

An unusual flower that blooms in sun or shade. One of the best plants for butterflies.

Blue Porterflower in front with Cranberry Pentas in the background

General: The primary advantages of Blue Porterflower are its unique color and flower shape. Blue is one of the most unusual flower colors and very necessary to provide contrast in the garden. The butterflies love Blue Porterflower, and it blooms in sun or shade. This plant is very easy to grow, although it requires a lot of trimming for a manicured look. Let it take its natural form, and trim it once or twice a year. Blue Porterflower has the look of a wildflower.

Companions: For an easy shade garden, plant Angelwing Begonias as the back layer, Yellow Mussaendas in the middle and border with Blue Porterflowers. Another great shade combination: use Shrimp Plants as the back layer, Blue Porterflowers in the middle and border with Starburst Pentas. The best of the butterfly companions are shown below.

Best of the butterfly plants

Jatropha

Golden Senna

Firebush

Firespike

Cassia Tree

Blue Porterflower

Cranberry Pentas

GROWING CONDITIONS

LIGHT: Medium shade to full sun. Grows thicker and blooms more in high light but is a very acceptable shade plant.

WATER: After initial establishment period, low water. Ideal is once a week in sun or wind or once every week or two in shade. Tolerates irrigation up to 3 times a week. Survives without irrigation in average environmental conditions.

SOIL: Wide range, if well drained.

SALT TOLERANCE: Medium

WIND TOLERANCE: Medium

ZONE: 10a to 11. To 32 deg. F.

PEST PROBLEMS: None serious.

PROPAGATION: Cuttings. Reseeds like a wildflower.

Care in the Landscape: Blue Porterflower requires frequent trimming for a neat look. For a wild flower look, it requires infrequent trimming, about once or twice a year. It recovers well from a hard cutback in the summer. Although not demanding of nutrition, it appreciates fertilization in March, June, and October with a well-balanced, slow-release mix with minor elements.

Botanical Name: *Tabernaemontana sp.*

Common Name: **Pinwheel Jasmine**

CHARACTERISTICS

PLANT TYPE: Shrub

AVERAGE SIZE: Easily maintained at sizes between 3 feet tall by 3 feet wide and 6 feet tall by 5 feet wide.

GROWTH RATE: Medium

LEAF: Glossy dark green; pointed, about 3 inches long.

FLOWER: White, shaped like a pinwheel, about 1 1/2 inches wide.

BEST COLOR: Blooms intermittently throughout the year, with most color in the warm months.

AVERAGE LIFE: 5 to 12 years.

ORIGIN: Unknown, but probably India.

CAUTIONS: None known

SPACING: 2 1/2 to 3 feet on center.

An attractive shrub with dark green, shiny leaves and pretty white flowers. Very easy to grow.

Pinwheel Jasmine in full flower

General: Plants with white flowers are generally weaker than plants with flowers of other colors. Not so for Pinwheel Jasmine. It is very attractive and easy to grow but is frequently misused as a sheared hedge. Pinwheel Jasmine stops flowering with frequent shearing. Let it grow naturally, and it becomes a welcome addition to the low maintenance garden.

Companions: Pinwheel Jasmine is predominately used in masses. I have also seen it used successfully as a single specimen. It works best as a specimen if the trunk shows because the trunk develops an interesting character as it ages. Some good shrub companions include Ixora Nora Grant and Snowbush.

Pinwheel Jasmine

Snowbush

Ixora Nora Grant

Close-up of Pinwheel Jasmine with some companions

Care in the Landscape: Fertilize Pinwheel Jasmine in March, June, and October with a well-balanced, slow-release mix with minor elements. If the plant looks yellowish all over, fertilize again, particularly in August. Trim once or twice a year, when it has stopped blooming. Pinwheel Jasmine is a much better bloomer if it is maintained in the four foot or higher range. Do not attempt to keep it under three feet, or it will eventually turn to sticks without flowers.

Botanical Name: *Viburnum suspensum*

Common Name: **Viburnum**

CHARACTERISTICS

PLANT TYPE: Most commonly used as a shrub.

AVERAGE SIZE: Easily maintained at sizes between 2 feet tall by 1 1/2 feet wide and 8 feet tall and 4 feet wide.

GROWTH RATE: Medium

LEAF: Olive green; about 3 inches long by 1 inch wide.

FLOWER: Insignificant

BEST COLOR: No seasonal variation.

AVERAGE LIFE: More than 20 years.

ORIGIN: India

CAUTIONS: Occasional unpleasant smell.

SPACING: 18 inches on center is the most common spacing for a hedge. If placed 24 inches on center, it will eventually grow together.

One of the best hedge materials available in south Florida. Compact growth in sun or partial shade. Long life-span with very little care.

Viburnum hedge with a border of Red Pentas

General: Viburnum is used primarily as a hedge. It offers much less maintenance than the more common Ficus because it grows more slowly. Viburnum is remarkably easy. I have never seen nutritional problems with this plant. It seems perfectly suited to south Florida soils. Many hedge plants thrive only in sun, which can be quite a problem if you need a hedge that spans both sunny and shady areas. Viburnum is equally at home in sun or shade.

Companions: Viburnum layers well with other hedge materials, like Silver Buttonwood, Lakeview Jasmine, and Cocoplum.

Close-up of Viburnum leaf

Viburnum viewed from above

GROWING CONDITIONS

LIGHT: Medium shade to full sun.

WATER: After initial establishment period, low water. Ideal is once a week. Tolerates irrigation as much as 5 or 6 times a week. Survives without irrigation in average environmental conditions.

SOIL: Wide range

SALT TOLERANCE: Low

WIND TOLERANCE: Medium

ZONE: 8 to 10b

PEST PROBLEMS: No major pests in the landscape.

PROPAGATION: Cuttings or seeds.

<u>Care in the Landscape:</u> Viburnum is very easy to grow. I have had it in one area of my trial garden for four years without trimming or fertilization. For a manicured look, trim it as needed, about three times per year. It benefits and grows faster with fertilization in March, June, and October with a well-balanced, slow-release mix with minor elements.

Botanical Name: *Zamia furfuracea*

Common Name: **Cardboard Palm**

CHARACTERISTICS

PLANT TYPE: Shrub, cycad

AVERAGE SIZE: 4 to 5 feet tall by 4 to 5 feet wide. Cannot be maintained smaller.

GROWTH RATE: Slow

LEAF: Dark olive green; about 1 inch wide by 6 inches long. Arranged on a center stem like a fern.

FLOWER: Cone

BEST COLOR: No seasonal variation.

AVERAGE LIFE: At least 25 years.

ORIGIN: Mexico

CAUTIONS: Poisonous

SPACING: 3 to 4 feet on center.

An easy specimen for a tropical garden. Big impact with very little care.

Close-up of a Cardboard Palm

General: The Cardboard Palm is an old plant that is making a comeback. It is an excellent substitute for the Sago Palm, which is falling victim to the Cycad Scale. It offers tropical texture with little care. The Cardboard Palm is frequently misused as a small accent. This is a large plant and cannot be maintained at smaller than four feet by four feet.

Companions: Use the Cardboard Palm with tropical textures, such as palms, Xanadus, Ti Plants, and Crotons.

Right (Before): A lonely Sago Palm is diseased with Cycad Scale. Alexander Palms mark the corners.

Below (After): The Cardboard Palm is the plant to the left, followed by a Fire Dragon Acalypha, and a European Fan Palm. Juniper is the border. Notice how much better the house looks.

Before

After

GROWING CONDITIONS

LIGHT: Medium shade to full sun.

WATER: After initial establishment period, low water. Ideal is once a week in sun or wind or once every other week in shade. Tolerates irrigation up to 5 times a week. Survives without irrigation in average environmental conditions.

SOIL: Wide range

SALT TOLERANCE: High

WIND TOLERANCE: Medium

ZONE: 9b to 11

PEST PROBLEMS: Few pests in the landscape; occasional scale and mealybugs.

PROPAGATION: Seeds

Care in the Landscape: The Cardboard Palm is very easy to grow. It benefits and grows faster from fertilization in March, June, and October with a well-balanced, slow-release mix that contains minor elements. The only trimming required is to remove the dead fronds that appear occasionally at the base.

CHAPTER 3

VINES

MOST TROPICAL VINES ARE FAST GROWING, RE-QUIRING TRIMMING MUCH MORE THAN THE THREE-TIMES-PER-YEAR MAXIMUM FOR THIS BOOK. HOW-EVER, VINES ARE AN IMPORTANT ELEMENT OF TODAY'S LANDSCAPES. SINCE THE GOAL OF THIS BOOK IS A COMPLETE PLANT PALETTE FOR MOST RESIDENCES, FOUR VINES ARE INCLUDED. THESE VINES ARE SOME OF THE EASIEST THAT ARE CUR-RENTLY AVAILABLE FOR SOUTH FLORIDA.

Left and above: Confederate Jasmine climbs the columns to the left as well as the Sabal Palms above.

Botanical Name: *Clerodendrum thomsoniae*

Common Name: **Bleeding Heart Vine**

CHARACTERISTICS

PLANT TYPE: Vine

AVERAGE SIZE: Exact size at maturity unknown. On the small size for south Florida vines. Covers a trellis about 6 feet tall by 3 feet wide.

GROWTH RATE: Medium

LEAF: Dark green; pointed, about 3 to 6 inches long by 1 inch wide.

FLOWER: White and red hanging cluster.

BEST COLOR: In zones 10 and 11, blooms off and on all year, including winter. In zone 9, it dies back in winter and blooms in summer.

AVERAGE LIFE: 5 to 10 years.

ORIGIN: West Africa

CAUTIONS: None known

SPACING: 3 to 4 feet on center.

A beautiful flower on an easy vine that blooms in sun or shade. A small vine, ideal for small trellises.

Bleeding Heart flowers hang in clusters at the ends of the branches. The flower is distinctive because it is two colors.

General: The Bleeding Heart Vine is an excellent choice when a smaller vine is needed. Most tropical vines are capable of covering a forest in a single season. Not so for the Bleeding Heart. It is quite well-behaved and the smallest vine in this book. It is a good candidate for arches and small trellises mounted on walls. Some trim it into a shrub, but this practice requires a lot of maintenance. Boasting an almost continuous bloom cycle, the Bleeding Heart is equally happy in sun or shade, providing the shade is not dense.

Companions: Bleeding Heart is versatile both in its light requirements and its style. It blends well with most other plants. A good combination for a shade garden includes Bleeding Hearts on a trellis behind Firespikes, followed by Ruellia Purple Showers and Shrimp Plants. Alternate the Shrimp and Ruellia and border with Blue Daze.

Bleeding Heart Vine

Shrimp Plant   *Ruellia Purple Showers*   *Firespike*

Close-up of Bleeding Heart flower with some companions

Care in the Landscape: The Bleeding Heart is a medium feeder. Fertilize in March, June, and October with a well-balanced, slow-release mix with minor elements. If the leaves turn yellowish in-between the veins, fertilize again. Be sure that the mix includes minor elements. Trim the Bleeding Heart as needed; once or twice a year is usually sufficient.

GROWING CONDITIONS

LIGHT: Low, medium, or high. Does not flower in dense shade. Prefers medium shade.

WATER: After initial establishment, medium. Ideal is once a week in shade or twice a week in sun or wind. Tolerates irrigation at least as much as 4 times a week. Untested without irrigation.

SOIL: Wide range, as long as it is well drained.

SALT TOLERANCE: Low

WIND TOLERANCE: Unknown

ZONE: 9 to 11; dies back in a freeze and re-sprouts the next spring.

PEST PROBLEMS: No frequent problems in the landscape. Occasional mites and nematodes.

PROPAGATION: Cuttings or seeds.

Botanical Name: *Passiflora spp.*

Common Name: **Passion Flower Vine**

CHARACTERISTICS

PLANT TYPE: Vine

AVERAGE SIZE: Variable. This is an extremely large vine. Plant it and stand back.

GROWTH RATE: Fast

LEAF: Medium green; variable in size and shape.

FLOWER: Many colors available, including red, blue, purple, white, and yellowish green. Sizes range from tiny 1/4 inch to large, spectacular 4 inch specimen. I only tested the red and purple, which are the ones more commonly available in the nurseries.

BEST COLOR: Red Passion Flower blooms in the late fall, winter and spring. Purple Passion Vine peaks in the warm months.

AVERAGE LIFE: At least 10 years.

ORIGIN: South America

CAUTIONS: Keep away from trees. This vine grows so aggressively that it can cover a tree and kill it. If one threatens a tree, cut the bottom stalk where it goes into the ground to kill the vine rather than the tree.

SPACING: 6 to 8 feet on center.

Spectacular flower on a fast-growing, large-scale vine. The purple is one of our best butterfly plants.

Red Passion Flower (Passiflora coccinea)

General: Passion Flower vines produce fabulous flowers. They are large-scale plants and, for years, I never recommended them for a low-maintenance garden for fear that they would escape their bounds and overtake all the other plants. Then, I learned how easy they are to remove (see 'CAUTIONS' on this page) and began liberally using them with good success. They are great for covering fences, especially if you mix the colors. Since the different colors bloom at different times, mixing the colors gives almost continuous blooms. Passion Flowers are great favorites of wildlife, attracting many bumblebees and butterflies. The purple is a larval plant for many Florida butterflies, which lay their eggs on the leaves. When the caterpillars hatch, they eat the leaves (see 'PEST PROBLEMS', opposite).

Companions: To attract butterflies, plant Purple Passion Flowers with Pentas, Jatropha, Blue Porterflower, and Firebush. Passion Flowers are too big for small arches. Use them on larger pergolas or to cover fences. For a large area, alternate purple and red Passion Flower Vines.

Purple Passion Flower (Passiflora caerulea)

Care in the Landscape: Passion Flower vines are not demanding of food. If fed with too much nitrogen, the vines will grow faster without producing flowers. Fertilize lightly in March, June, and October with a well-balanced, slow-release mix with minor elements. If well mulched, the vines may not need fertilizer. If the leaves turn yellowish, this is a signal that the plant is hungry. Place the plant so that it can grow quite large, or trimming will become a chore (see 'CAUTIONS' on the opposite page). Trim as needed after the plant has finished a bloom cycle.

GROWING CONDITIONS

LIGHT: High

WATER: After initial establishment period, low. Ideal is once a week. Tolerates irrigation up to 3 times a week. Survives without irrigation in average environmental conditions.

SOIL: Wide range

SALT TOLERANCE: Purple Passion Flower (Passiflora caerulea) is medium. The red and other purples are low.

WIND TOLERANCE: Unknown

ZONE: Red, 10b to 11; Purple, 9 to 11.

PEST PROBLEMS: Red Passion vines have few pests. Purple Passion vines are the larval food for many butterflies. I consider them pet food in my garden. The butterflies lay their eggs on the bottoms of the leaves. When the eggs hatch into caterpillars, the little caterpillars eat the leaves. Please never spray a Purple Passion vine with pesticides because of the danger of killing future butterflies. The caterpillars that eat the leaves do not spread onto other plants or kill the vine.

PROPAGATION: Cuttings

Botanical Name: *Petrea volubilis*

Common Name: **Queen's Wreath, Tropical Wisteria**

CHARACTERISTICS

PLANT TYPE: Vine

AVERAGE SIZE: Variable; a medium-sized vine.

GROWTH RATE: Medium

LEAF: Medium green; about 4 inches long. Feels rough, like light sandpaper.

FLOWER: Purple or white; spectacular hanging clusters about 8 to 10 inches long.

BEST COLOR: In most years, peaks for about 6 weeks in February and March, with sporadic blooms in the spring and fall.

AVERAGE LIFE: At least 10 years.

ORIGIN: Caribbean Region

CAUTIONS: None known

SPACING: 4 to 6 feet on center.

Petrea is one of the most beautiful flowers in south Florida. It resembles the northern plant, Wisteria.

Petrea in full bloom on an arbor

General: Petrea is a little-used plant that is spectacular, but it is slow to begin blooming. Once I recommended it for climbing a trellis on either side of a client's garage. Three years after planting, she told me she almost wrecked her car after noticing the first blooms. Nurseries are now stocking older plants so, unless you are very patient, buy a big one. Petrea is a large vine that is ideal for large trellises and arbors. Its bottom branches become quite thick and woody. The blooms appear on top.

Companions: Petrea blends well with all landscape styles. Combine it with pinks and yellows. Some good companions for under an arbor covered with Petrea include Angelwing Begonia and Walking Iris.

Petrea

Angelwing Begonia

Walking Iris

Close-up of Petrea flower with some companions

Care in the Landscape: Petrea is not demanding of care. Fertilize in March, June, and October with a well-balanced, slow-release mix that contains minor elements. Trim when it is not blooming to keep it within bounds.

Botanical Name: *Trachelospermum jasminoides*

Common Name: **Confederate Jasmine**

CHARACTERISTICS

PLANT TYPE: Vine

AVERAGE SIZE: Variable. A medium-sized vine.

GROWTH RATE: Medium

LEAF: Dark, glossy green; about 1 to 2 inches long.

FLOWER: White; about 1 inch across. Fragrant.

BEST COLOR: Spring; blooming lasts about 2 months.

AVERAGE LIFE: At least 10 years.

ORIGIN: China

CAUTIONS: None known

SPACING: 3 to 4 feet on center.

A lovely white flower on an easy vine that blooms in sun or shade. Wonderful scent.

Confederate Jasmine in full bloom

General: Confederate Jasmine is one of south Florida's most dependable plants for scent. And, unlike many tropical vines, it is quite controllable. Although the bloom period is short, the attractive, dark green leaves look good, even when the plant is not blooming. It is among the few plants that is well adapted to extremes of temperature, thriving in the warmth of south Florida, as well as the freezes of north Florida.

Companions: If planting in front of Confederate Jasmine, use plants that show up against the dark green leaves. Other plants with similar leaves will not work well. Snowbush is an excellent choice, along with Croton and Ti Plant. If using this Jasmine on an arch, any plant works well in the same garden.

Confederate Jasmine growing up a Sabal Palm. Do not allow it to cover the palm fronds or it could kill the palm.

Care in the Landscape: Confederate Jasmine is easy to grow, provided it has good air circulation and decent soil. If the air is stagnant, it develops scale and sooty mold. It is not a heavy feeder but grows faster and better if fertilized in March, June, and October with a well-balanced, slow-release mix with minor elements. Trim as needed in summer or fall to keep within bounds.

GROWING CONDITIONS

LIGHT: Medium to high

WATER: After initial establishment period, medium water. Ideal is twice a week. Tolerates irrigation at least as much as 3 times a week. Untested without irrigation.

SOIL: Wide range

SALT TOLERANCE: Medium

WIND TOLERANCE: Medium

ZONE: 8 to 10b

PEST PROBLEMS: Scale and sooty mold. Fewer pests in areas of medium to high light and good air circulation. Not recommended for under screening.

PROPAGATION: Cuttings

CHAPTER 4

SMALL TREES, 8 TO 15 FEET TALL

*Left and above: Starburst or Shooting Star
(Clerodendrum quadriloculare)*

Botanical Name: *Breynia disticha*

Common Name: **Snowbush Tree or Standard**

CHARACTERISTICS

PLANT TYPE: Small tree or shrub. See pages 64 and 65 for information on the shrub.

AVERAGE SIZE: Easily maintained at sizes between 6 feet tall by 4 feet wide and 8 feet tall by 5 feet wide.

GROWTH RATE: Medium

LEAF: Small (about 1/2 inch) and multicolored in shades of pink, red, green, and white.

FLOWER: Inconspicuous

BEST COLOR: All year, but winter cold can cause the leaves to darken somewhat. Brighter in summer.

AVERAGE LIFE: Unknown. The shrub lives for 5 to 10 years. I do not have more than 5 years' experience with the tree.

ORIGIN: Pacific Islands

CAUTIONS: Reproduces vigorously through underground runners.

SPACING: 5 feet on center

A plant that is usually grown as a shrub but forms a small tree if properly trained. Unique, colorful, and very useful in the small garden.

Snowbush Tree or standard with Sago Palm and Liriope

General: This tree is called Snowbush because its leaves resemble snow. Like Hibiscus, it is technically a shrub that can be trained into a small tree. I hesitated to use it for many years because I had heard it was invasive, producing so many runners that it became a nuisance. Extensive experience has shown me otherwise. It does send out runners but not enough to become a problem, provided they are pulled out annually.

Seminole Pink Hibiscus   *Pinwheel Jasmine*   *Cranberry Pentas*

Some companions

Companions: Snowbush combines beautifully with plants that have white or pink to red flowers. Use it as a tall accent, with Pinwheel Jasmine behind it and Cranberry Pentas in front. Snowbush Tree is also beautiful when planted with a pair of Seminole Pink Hibiscus trees, one on each side. Jatropha Trees also make good companions. Liriope is an excellent groundcover with Snowbush, as shown opposite.

Close-up of Snowbush leaves

Care in the Landscape: Snowbush is very easy to maintain. Fertilize in March, June, and October with a well-balanced, slow-release mix that contains minor elements. Trim as needed to control size. Trim off any shoots that appear on the bare part of the trunk. Remove any sprouts as you would a weed.

GROWING CONDITIONS

LIGHT: Full sun. More colorful and dense in high light. Fades completely in shade.

WATER: After initial establishment period, medium water. Ideal is twice a week. Tolerates irrigation at least as often as 4 times a week. Untested without irrigation.

SOIL: Wide range

SALT TOLERANCE: Medium

WIND TOLERANCE: Low

ZONE: 10b to 11. Survives 32 deg. F. Foliage darkens and its brightness fades somewhat in response to temperatures under about 42 deg. F.

PEST PROBLEMS: At the time of writing this book, I question Snowbush as a low maintenance plant because of severe caterpillar infestations. During the 90's, I only witnessed occasional caterpillar attacks. In the summer of 2000, I heard of many. These attacks are severe enough to completely defoliate the plant. The caterpillar is easily controlled by spraying but the plants in this book are relatively pest resistent naturally. I include Snowbush in this book with the hope that the frequency of the attacks is an exception and not the norm.

PROPAGATION: Easily reproduced from cuttings or runners.

Botanical Name: *Clerodendrum quadriloculare*

Common Name: **Starburst or Shooting Star**

CHARACTERISTICS

PLANT TYPE: Small tree or large shrub.

AVERAGE SIZE: Easily maintained at sizes between 6 feet tall by 5 feet wide and 10 feet tall by 8 feet wide.

GROWTH RATE: Fast

LEAF: Olive green on top and purple on bottom. Sizes of the leaves vary from about 3 to 6 inches long.

FLOWER: Spectacular clusters of white flowers that resemble stars with light pink throats. Clusters measure a full 12 inches across.

BEST COLOR: Leaf color lasts all year. Flowers appear in late winter, January or February, occasionally as late as March. Although the flowers last only about 6 weeks, they are spectacular. The plant is quite attractive when not in bloom.

AVERAGE LIFE: Unknown because it is a recent introduction. May be short-lived, in the 5 to 10 year range.

ORIGIN: The only reference I could find is from Menninger's *Flowering Trees of the World*. He reports it growing commonly in Manila.

SPACING: 6 to 8 feet on center.

Wonderful flower on a fast-growing, large-scale shrub or small tree. One of the most spectacular plants in this book.

Starburst in full bloom

General: Starburst is a fabulous plant. It is technically a shrub, but most use it as a small tree because of its large size. It offers the advantages of low maintenance, year-round color (the leaf color lasts all year) and spectacular flowers. It is also quite economical because of its fast growth. Buy a three foot specimen and expect a six to eight foot specimen within the first year. Homeowners with Shooting Stars have told me that people frequently stop and ask them about it when it blooms. Golf course superintendents have told me that it is the favorite flowering tree of their golfers. Like many Clerodendrums, it sends up offshoots (see 'CAUTIONS', opposite).

Companions: In large spaces, plant Starbursts in groups of three, on about twelve foot centers, to give the effect of three separate plants. For screening, plant as a hedge, on about six foot centers. Starburst hedges are one of the most dramatic plant masses I have ever seen. For other companions, try Snowbush in sun or Angelwing Begonia in shade.

Close-up of Starburst flower. These spectacular clusters often measure a full 12 inches across.

Care in the Landscape: Starbursts are easy to grow. They are not demanding of fertilizer but benefit and grow faster from applications in March, June, and October with a well-balanced, slow-release mix that contains minor elements. Cut back the Starburst in April and again in August. Do not cut back after August, or it might not flower the following winter. Starbursts are difficult to maintain with a single trunk. Let them grow multiple trunks and trim off the unwanted branches at the bottom of the trunks to make them appear more treelike. Pull out unwanted suckers at the base.

Botanical Name: *Hibiscus 'Anderson Crepe'*

Common Name: **Anderson Crepe Hibiscus**

CHARACTERISTICS

PLANT TYPE: Small tree or shrub.

AVERAGE SIZE: Easily maintained at sizes between 7 feet tall by 5 feet wide and 12 feet tall by 8 feet wide.

GROWTH RATE: Fast

LEAF: Medium green; about 1 inch long. Smaller than many other varieties of Hibiscus.

FLOWER: Light pink, about 3 inches wide. White variety available as well.

BEST COLOR: Flowers on and off for most of the year.

AVERAGE LIFE: At least 20 years.

ORIGIN: China

CAUTIONS: Not a good candidate over pavement or pools because the flowers stick and are difficult to remove. Falls over easily and requires secure staking.

SPACING: 6 to 15 feet on center.

Flowers more than any other Hibiscus variety in our trials. Sometimes used as a shrub. Makes a fabulous small flowering tree as well.

Mature Anderson Crepe Hibiscus

General: Although the Anderson Crepe Hibiscus is technically a shrub, it makes a great flowering tree if trained to grow from a single trunk when young. This tree not only blooms more than most other Hibiscus varieties, but also is less susceptible to pests and nutritional deficiencies. Larger than most Hibiscus, its trunk develops a diameter of five to six inches. Weeping in habit, it is an excellent specimen for the south Florida garden. Its flowers are not as large as many other Hibiscus, but it flowers much more often, with a high percentage of color.

Companions: Plant it as a specimen or in groups. It is also a very attractive street tree. In the garden, the weeping form of this pink Hibiscus works well with other light textures. Its pink color contrasts well with yellows and blues. Thryallis, Plumbago, and Pentas make excellent companions. Snowbush is another good choice. Blue Daze forms an excellent border around a garden that includes the Anderson Crepe Hibiscus.

Before

Recently planted Hibiscus underplanted with Thryallis, Pentas, Blue Daze, and Yellow Lantana. Notice how nice the tree looks against the blue fence. The fence was originally an ugly gray color and covered with weeds (above). A simple coat of paint and some new plants transformed the area.

After

GROWING CONDITIONS

LIGHT: Light shade to full sun.

WATER: After initial establishment, medium water. Ideal is twice a week. Tolerates irrigation up to 3 times a week. Untested without irrigation.

SOIL: Wide range, if well drained. Will not tolerate wet feet. This variety of Hibiscus does not need acidic soil as much as others. It thrives on the native alkaline soils of south Florida.

SALT TOLERANCE: Medium

WIND TOLERANCE: Foliage has medium wind tolerance. Roots are shallow and tree may blow over unless staked. Many Anderson Crepes are staked the entire time they live if in a windy situation.

ZONE: 10a to 11. Survives 32 deg. F.

PEST PROBLEMS: Aphids and scale. This variety of Hibiscus had no pests at all in our trials. Many other varieties of Hibiscus were covered with pests, especially aphids.

PROPAGATION: Cuttings

Care in the Landscape: Keep small branches trimmed off the trunk and remove suckers that grow from the ground. Cut out crossed branches, but let all others grow long enough to weep. Do not trim this plant into a lollipop shape. It will look silly with a cluster of branches that stick straight up. Even out the branches at the bottom of the canopy, as shown in the mature specimen opposite. Fertilize in March, June, and October with a well-balanced, slow-release mix that contains minor elements.

Botanical Name: *Hibiscus rosa-sinensis 'Seminole Pink'*

Common Name: **Seminole Pink Hibiscus**

CHARACTERISTICS

PLANT TYPE: Shrub or small tree.

AVERAGE SIZE: Easily maintained at sizes between 6 feet tall by 5 feet wide and 9 feet tall by 7 feet wide.

GROWTH RATE: Fast

LEAF: Medium green; about 2 inches long.

FLOWER: Light pink, about 4 to 6 inches across.

BEST COLOR: Flowers on and off most of the year.

AVERAGE LIFE: 10 to 20 years.

ORIGIN: China

CAUTIONS: Not a good candidate over pavement or pools because the flowers stick and are difficult to remove. Falls over easily and requires secure staking.

SPACING: 6 to 12 feet on center.

An excellent choice for large flowers and a manicured form.

Mature Seminole Pink Hibiscus Tree

General: The Seminole Pink Hibiscus is one of the most colorful and easiest of all the Hibiscus. Like other Hibiscus, it grows as a shrub but makes an excellent small tree when trained to grow from a single trunk when young. Since it is a strong variety of Hibiscus, it does not suffer from as many nutritional deficiencies and pest problems as many other kinds of Hibiscus. It does not flower as profusely as the Anderson Crepe, but its flowers are larger. It is an upright grower as compared with the weeping habit of the Anderson Crepe. The leggy habit of this shrub makes it easier to maintain as a small tree than as a shrub.

Companions: For a small tree grouping, plant this Hibiscus near *Senna surattensis* and Jatropha. Shrubs that work well under this Hibiscus include Snowbush, Plumbago, and Pentas. Blue Daze forms an excellent groundcover under this tree.

Close-up of the Seminole Hibiscus flower

Care in the Landscape: This Hibiscus needs room to spread, at least five feet for adequate flowering. The most common mistake with Hibiscus is trimming them too small or too often to bloom. Many shear Hibiscus monthly into a hedge and wonder why it never flowers. Trim infrequently but make deep cuts instead of just knocking off the tips each month. This manner allows each branch to grow long enough to produce flowers. Trim once or twice a year, immediately after it has bloomed. Keep the small branches trimmed off the trunk and remove any suckers (small branches) that appear from the ground. Remove any crossed branches. Fertilize in March, June, and October with a well-balanced, slow-release mix that includes minor elements.

GROWING CONDITIONS

LIGHT: Light shade to full sun.

WATER: After initial establishment, medium water. Ideal is twice a week. Tolerates irrigation up to 3 times a week. Untested without irrigation.

SOIL: Wide range, if well drained, but will not tolerate wet feet. Thrives in a slightly acidic soil but performs acceptably well in native alkaline soils.

SALT TOLERANCE: Medium

WIND TOLERANCE: Foliage has medium wind tolerance. Roots are shallow and have low wind tolerance unless staked.

ZONE: 10a to 11

PEST PROBLEMS: Scales or aphids occasionally.

PROPAGATION: Cuttings

Botanical Name: *Jatropha integerrima 'Compacta'*

Common Name: **Jatropha**

CHARACTERISTICS

PLANT TYPE: Small tree or shrub. See pages 90 and 91 for shrub information.

AVERAGE SIZE: Easily maintained at sizes between 6 feet tall by 6 feet wide and 10 feet tall by 7 feet wide.

GROWTH RATE: Medium

LEAF: Deep green; about 4 inches long. The shapes vary from fiddle-shaped to oval, often on the same plant. The old Jatropha (not the 'Compacta' variety) have all oval leaves.

FLOWER: Most are red. Some tend toward orange or pink. Individual blooms are 1 inch long in clusters.

BEST COLOR: Blooms all year but more profusely in the warmer months.

AVERAGE LIFE: 10 to 30 years.

ORIGIN: Cuba and South America.

CAUTIONS: Poisonous

SPACING: 5 to 8 feet on center.

One of the few small trees that blooms every day of the year. A great butterfly plant. One of the few flowering trees that can be maintained at such a small size.

A mature Jatropha Tree

General: Jatropha grows as a shrub or small tree (standard), depending on how it was trimmed when young. The plant is easier to grow as a tree because it has a tendency towards legginess as a shrub. It offers the advantages of constant blooms with very little care. Very few plants actually bloom 365 days a year. Most need a rest at some point. Not so for Jatropha. It keeps producing blooms, no matter what the weather. The new 'Compacta' variety is far superior to the older Jatropha, which is more loose and leggy. Jatropha is a great plant for butterflies. When we first brought plants into our test garden, the butterflies went for the Jatropha first, particularly the Zebra butterfly.

Companions: For small flowering tree companions, consider Anderson Crepe Hibiscus and Golden Senna. They make a lovely grouping of three. Shrimp Plants, Plumbagos, and Pentas are good choices for under Jatropha trees. Mammey Crotons are another great choice for underneath Jatropha.

Close-up of Jatropha flower

Recently planted Jatropha

Care in the Landscape:

Prune once a year. It is difficult to give an ideal time to prune because pruning is generally done when a tree has just finished flowering. Since Jatropha never stops flowering, trimming can be done any time of year. I prune mine in the fall because Jatrophas bloom more in summer, and a fall pruning produces more branch tips for the following summer. Fertilize in March, June, and October with a well-balanced, slow-release mix that contains minor elements.

Botanical Name: *Murraya paniculata 'Lakeview'*

Common Name: **Lakeview Jasmine, Orange Jasmine**

CHARACTERISTICS

PLANT TYPE: Small tree or shrub. For shrub information, see pages 92 and 93.

AVERAGE SIZE: Easily maintained at sizes between 6 feet tall by 5 feet wide and 15 feet tall by 10 feet wide.

GROWTH RATE: Medium

LEAF: Dark, glossy green; about 3/4 inch long.

FLOWER: White, fragrant, round clusters about 1 inch in diameter.

BEST COLOR: Flowers on and off throughout the year. Does not bloom as long as most of the flowering plants in this book, about 3 months per year. Worth planting for its form and scent.

AVERAGE LIFE: 10 to 20 years.

ORIGIN: Asia, Australia and the Pacific Islands.

CAUTIONS: Attracts bees

SPACING: 6 to 10 feet on center.

A great tree for small spots. Easy to maintain with a wonderful scent.

Lakeview Jasmine Standard (Tree)

General: The single biggest mistake I see in residential plantings is large shade trees in small spots, particularly Oaks and Mahoganies. These trees spread about 50 feet and are frequently planted in about six feet of space. The Lakeview Jasmine is an ideal and under-used tree for these small spaces. It grows as a shrub, if not trimmed into a tree, and is very trainable. The Lakeview Jasmine is not only very well-formed and attractive, but very easy to grow. It also boasts the wonderful scent of Jasmine. Lakeview Jasmine is an improved variety of the old Orange Jasmine, offering slightly larger leaves and flowers.

Companions: Lakeview Jasmine works well as a street tree, especially under power lines. It is adaptive to many landscape styles, as appropriate in a cottage garden as in a manicured garden. Other small trees that look good with Lakeview Jasmine include Jatropha and Seminole Pink Hibiscus, which have similar tight forms. Snowbush Trees are also attractive on either side of a Lakeview Jasmine Tree.

Small Lakeview Jasmine tree planted in a container.

Close-up of flower

Care in the Landscape: Remove any small branches that appear on the trunk. Remove any crossed branches in the canopy. If trimmed too often, Lakeview Jasmine will not flower, so trim the canopy right after it stops blooming. Trim no more than once or twice a year for optimum blooming. Fertilize in March, June, and October with a well-balanced, slow-release mix with minor elements. Lakeview Jasmine sometimes shows nutritional deficiencies in poor soils, shown by yellow leaves. Fertilize again in August if this occurs.

GROWING CONDITIONS

LIGHT: Light shade to full sun. Flowers more in full sun but flowers acceptably in light shade as well. Not for dense shade.

WATER: After initial establishment, low water. Once a week is ideal. Tolerates irrigation at least up to 3 times a week. Untested without irrigation.

SOIL: If soils are poor, this plant requires more fertilizer than most in this book. Does very well in most south Florida neighborhoods. I have noticed the most problems in new neighborhoods with poor fill soil, particularly soil with a lot of shellrock.

SALT TOLERANCE: Medium

WIND TOLERANCE: Medium

ZONE: 9 to 11. Dies back at 30 deg. F. but recovers.

PEST PROBLEMS: Few pests in the landscape. We had none in our trials. I have heard reports of occasional whiteflies, sooty mold, scale, or nematodes.

PROPAGATION: Cuttings or seeds.

Botanical Name: *Senna polyphylla*

Common Name: **Golden Senna, Desert Cassia**

A superior plant that, not only is among the few that stays small, but also has a long bloom period, beautiful weeping form, and attracts butterflies.

CHARACTERISTICS

PLANT TYPE: Small tree

AVERAGE SIZE: Easily maintained at sizes between 7 to 9 feet tall by 5 to 6 feet wide. I have been watching this tree for 9 years, and this is as large as it has grown.

GROWTH RATE: Slow. Senna trees do not develop into full specimens in nursery pots. They need to be in the ground for about a year before they thicken up.

LEAF: Tiny and needlelike. Each leaf is about 1 inch long. Leaves grow on stems that give a feathery look.

FLOWER: Yellow; about 1 inch across, arranged in clusters.

BEST COLOR: Winter months. Blooms about half the year, in spurts. Flowers last a few weeks, take a rest, then return. Looks very good when not in bloom.

AVERAGE LIFE: Unknown. I have only been growing them for about 9 years. The ones that are 9 years old are still growing beautifully.

ORIGIN: Unknown

CAUTIONS: Produces seed pods that may seem unattractive. If bothered, just pull them off.

SPACING: 6 to 8 feet on center.

Golden Senna in bloom

General: The Golden Senna was chosen one of the plants of the year by the Florida Nurserymen and Growers Association for 1998. It deserves the title and then some. Truly good, small, flowering trees are few and far between, and the Senna is one of the best. It blooms for at least six months a year at the best time possible - winter - when people want to be outside enjoying the flowers. Its weeping form is very attractive, even when not blooming. And, it is very easy to grow.

Companions: Anderson Crepe Hibiscus is an excellent companion for Golden Senna because its weeping form is similar. They do not always bloom at the same time, but one is blooming most of the time. Jatropha trees look good with the Senna because the red contrasts nicely with the yellow. Underplant the Senna with low-growing materials, like Fire Crotons, Starburst Pentas, Dwarf Chenilles, or Ruellia Katies. Larger shrubs do not work well underneath because they grow so tall they hide the form of the tree.

Close-up of the Senna flower

Care in the Landscape: This is a very easy plant. It is not a heavy feeder but benefits and grows faster with fertilizations in March, June, and October with a well-balanced, slow-release mix containing minor elements. Remove any small branches that appear on the trunk, as well as any crossed branches. Trim the ends of the branches about every two years after it finishes blooming, normally in May or June. Trimming the branch tips thickens the tree and increases the number of flowers the following winter.

Botanical Name: *Senna surattensis*

Common Name: **Glaucous Cassia or Cassia Tree**

One of our best flowering trees. It has a long blooming period, is evergreen and is well-proportioned for smaller residences.

CHARACTERISTICS

PLANT TYPE: Small tree

AVERAGE SIZE: 10 to 15 feet tall by 6 to 8 feet wide.

GROWTH RATE: Fast

LEAF: Medium green; about 1 inch long by 1/2 inch wide. Leaves grow on long stems like a fern.

FLOWER: Very showy clusters of yellow flowers. Each flower is about 1 to 2 inches wide.

BEST COLOR: In most years, blooms for about 6 months in 2 spurts, one in fall and one in spring. Some years, blooms in summer and winter as well.

AVERAGE LIFE: Unknown. Tree is a fairly new introduction into the landscape trade. Old sources refer to a short life-span on some of the yellow Sennas.

ORIGIN: Southeast Asia, Australia.

CAUTIONS: Requires staking or falls over.

SPACING: 8 to 10 feet on center.

Senna surattensis in full bloom

General: The beautiful Glaucous Cassia has lovely flowers that last up to six months a year, which is much longer than most flowering trees. Not only is this Senna a strong bloomer, but, unlike many flowering trees, it is evergreen. Be sure to stake it securely when planting as it has a tendency to become top heavy. This tree used to be named *Cassia surattensis*.

Companions: This tree works well alone or in groups and blends well with many different styles. In a tree grouping, one of the best combinations includes this Senna, Jatropha, and Anderson Crepe Hibiscus. In a cottage garden, mix it with Pentas and Plumbago. For a tropical look, use this tree with Crotons, Ti Plants, Dwarf Jatrophas, White Birds of Paradise and palms.

Close-up of the flowers

Care in the Landscape: This tree sometimes needs structural pruning when young to keep it from growing like a shrub. Trim unwanted branches from the trunk, particularly those that grow low. Sometimes the canopy grows faster than the trunk, causing the tree to become top-heavy. If this occurs, thin out the canopy. The tree also needs staking to keep it from falling over. As the tree matures, little trimming is required. Fertilize in March, June, and October with a well-balanced, slow-release mix that contains minor elements.

Botanical Name: *Strelitzia nicolai*

Common Name: **White Bird of Paradise**

CHARACTERISTICS

PLANT TYPE: Small tree or large shrub.

AVERAGE SIZE: Easily maintained at sizes between 8 feet tall by 6 feet wide and 15 feet tall by 12 feet wide.

GROWTH RATE: Medium

LEAF: Medium green, banana-like; 6 feet long by 18 inches wide at maturity.

FLOWER: Looks like a bird. About 8 inches long. White on the top and blue on the bottom. Not as showy as the Orange Bird of Paradise. Sometimes hidden by the leaves. Although the flower is quite attractive, this plant is grown primarily for its foliage.

BEST COLOR: Blooms on and off throughout the year.

AVERAGE LIFE: More than 20 years.

ORIGIN: Africa

CAUTIONS: None known

SPACING: 6 to 12 feet on center.

Most big-leaf tropicals require much more care and water than this dependable plant.

Mature White Bird

General: Unlike the Orange Bird of Paradise, the White Bird is valued more for its foliage than its flower. Plants with large, banana-like leaf textures are an integral part of the tropical garden and are usually very water and maintenance intensive. The White Bird has the big-leaf texture without requiring much water or maintenance. It also has an unusual flat growth habit that is useful in many situations, particularly against walls and fences. The White Bird is also a good choice for pots. I once had one on a screened patio that I planted in a three foot square wooden planter. It lasted seven years in the same pot, which is much longer than most plants live in the same size container.

Companions: For a tropical look, plant the White Bird with Ti Plants, Crotons, and palms. The White Bird also blends well with flowering plants, like the Shrimp Plants, Angel-wing Begonias, and Firespikes.

Right: Close-up of the flower.

Care in the Landscape: The White Bird is not demanding of nutrition. It appreciates and grows faster when fertilized in March, June, and October with a well-balanced, slow-release mix with minor elements. Trim off any dead leaves or flowers as needed. If the plant gets too tall, trim the tallest trunk all the way to the ground. Most people trim the tallest leaves without removing the attached trunk at the ground.

Before

After

White Birds are frequently used in planters next to walls. Their narrow width is appropriate for this use. If the plant is trimmed correctly, it should last about 10 years in this location before it outgrows it.

LIGHT: Medium shade to full sun.

WATER: After initial establishment period, low water. Ideal is once or twice a week in sun or once every 10 days in shade. Tolerates irrigation at least as often as 4 times a week. Untested without irrigation.

SOIL: Wide range

SALT TOLERANCE: Medium

WIND TOLERANCE: Low

ZONE: 9 to 11. Tolerates temperatures down to 25 deg F.

PEST PROBLEMS: Scale is a frequent problem if the plant is indoors or under screening. Outside, the plant has few pests.

PROPAGATION: Seeds or suckers.

CHAPTER 5

MEDIUM TREES, 15 TO 35 FEET TALL

Left and above: Yellow Tabebuia (Tabebuia caraiba)

Botanical Name: *Conocarpus erectus var. sericeus*

Common Name: **Silver Buttonwood**

CHARACTERISTICS

PLANT TYPE: Medium tree or shrub. See pages 76 and 77 for information on shrub.

AVERAGE SIZE: Easily maintained at sizes between 8 feet tall by 6 feet wide and 20 feet tall by 15 feet wide.

GROWTH RATE: Medium

LEAF: Silver green; about 2 inches long.

FLOWER: Insignificant

BEST COLOR: No seasonal variation.

AVERAGE LIFE: 50 years

ORIGIN: South Florida and the West Indies.

CAUTIONS: None known

SPACING: 6 to 15 feet on center.

An excellent native tree for areas of high salt and wind. Silver leaf color is a good contrast with bright flowers or leaves. Easy to sculpt into smaller sizes.

Silver Buttonwood in Key West

General: Silver Buttonwood takes a lot of tough environments, especially salt, wind, and drought. Salt air keeps it free of aphids and sooty mold, two organisms that commonly inhabit the tree in non-salt situations. For years, I never recommended Silver Buttonwoods west of US1 on the east coast of Florida because of the lack of salt. The Silver Buttonwoods I saw in the western environments were black with sooty mold unless constantly sprayed. In recent years, however, I have seen more and more Silver Buttonwoods doing well in western Palm Beach County. The gnarled trunks of old Silver Buttonwoods add character to any setting. Buttonwoods are also available in a green form, which is more cold tolerant than the silver.

Companions: Silver Buttonwoods look best with bright colors. Purple Queen is one of the best companions. This combination is an excellent choice for color by the ocean. Crotons also contrast well with Silver Buttonwood. Ti Plants are a good companion when in a low salt environment.

Right: Silver Buttonwood trunks

Below: Close-up of the leaf

GROWING CONDITIONS

LIGHT: Full sun

WATER: After initial establishment period, low water. Ideal is once a week. Tolerates irrigation up to 3 times a week.

SOIL: Wide range

SALT TOLERANCE: High

WIND TOLERANCE: High

ZONE: 10b to 11. Some leaf drop at 40 deg.F.

PEST PROBLEMS: Sooty mold, scale, mites. These problems seldom occur close to the ocean.

PROPAGATION: Seeds or cuttings.

Care in the Landscape: Silver Buttonwood trees are very easy to grow. I have heard tree specialists refer to them as putty because they are so easy to mold to different sizes and shapes. Trim the small branches from the base of the trunk of small trees. They seldom appear on older specimens. If space allows, let the tree form naturally as it matures. Buttonwoods are accustomed to our native soils and seldom have to have fertilizer, but they benefit and grow faster with fertilization in March, June, and October with a well-balanced, slow-release mix that contains minor elements.

Botanical Name: *Cordia sebestena*

Common Name: **Orange Geiger**

CHARACTERISTICS

PLANT TYPE: Medium tree

AVERAGE SIZE: 20 feet tall by 15 feet wide.

GROWTH RATE: Medium

LEAF: Olive green, rough-textured; sizes vary a lot on different trees, from about 4 inches long by 2 inches wide to 8 inches long by 4 inches wide.

FLOWER: Orange, trumpet-shaped. Individual flowers are about 1 inch wide and grow in clusters.

BEST COLOR: Summer and fall.

AVERAGE LIFE: At least 50 years.

ORIGIN: South Florida and the West Indies.

CAUTIONS: Do not place this tree where it will be a focal point in winter. Also, the Geiger beetle can defoliate the tree. See 'PEST PROBLEMS' in the green column on the opposite page.

SPACING: 10 to 15 feet on center.

One of the few native trees that has showy flowers. A favorite food for Hummingbirds.

Geiger tree in june

General: The Orange Geiger is a wonderful flowering tree. It is native to the Keys and requires very little care. In the Keys, not many Geiger trees are visible in the wild because most have been removed. The Geiger deserves more use throughout south Florida. Its small size is ideal for residences. Because of cold sensitivity, its leaves do not look good in the winter. Yellow and White Geigers are also available, but their growth habits are quite different. Neither are native to south Florida. The White Geiger is much larger and has not thrived in our trials. The Yellow Geiger is smaller and has performed quite well in the first two years of our trials.

Companions: If many Geiger trees are planted together, the chances of defoliation by the Geiger beetle increase. Use the Geiger mixed with other native trees, like Silver Buttonwoods and Gumbo Limbos. It is also an excellent choice for gardens to attract wildlife. To attract Hummingbirds, plant with Firebush, Firespike, and the Shrimp Plant.

Close-up of the Geiger flower with some companions

Care in the Landscape: Orange Geigers are very easy, if the beetles are tolerated (see 'PEST PROBLEMS'). We planted two small specimens during the rainy season four years ago in our trial garden. They have thrived without any fertilizer, irrigation, or trimming. Do not try this in poor fill soil, during the dry season, or with a large specimen, as large specimens take more water to establish. Without supplemental fertilizer or water, Orange Geigers grow slowly.

GROWING CONDITIONS

LIGHT: Full sun. Geiger trees did not do well at all in even light shade in our trials.

WATER: After initial establishment period, low water. Ideal is once a week. Tolerates irrigation up to 3 times a week. Survives quite well without irrigation in average environmental conditions.

SOIL: Wide range, if well drained.

SALT TOLERANCE: High

WIND TOLERANCE: High

ZONE: 10b to 11. Survives 32 deg. F. with leaf damage but recovers quickly. Dies back to the ground in severe freezes.

PEST PROBLEMS: Geiger beetles are a major pest and are capable of completely defoliating the tree. They appear more on groups of Geigers than single specimens. The beetle does not kill the tree, simply eats the leaves. If chewed leaves are undesirable, consider locating the Geiger tree at a distance, where the flowers will show but the leaves will be less conspicuous. Some consider the beetle a bonus because it is quite beautiful, with iridescent colorations.

PROPAGATION: Air layers or seeds.

Botanical Name: *Filicium decipiens*

Common Name: **Japanese Fern Tree**

A beautiful tree with an interesting texture; useful because of its small size and very attractive appearance.

CHARACTERISTICS

PLANT TYPE: Medium tree

AVERAGE SIZE: Mature size is 30 feet tall by 20 feet wide. Can be maintained smaller by trimming. I have never tried to maintain it smaller than about 20 feet tall by 15 feet wide. Since I have seen it growing as a hedge, it stands to reason that it is a very controllable plant.

GROWTH RATE: Medium

LEAF: Medium green; about 2 inches long arranged on a stem like a fern.

FLOWER: Inconspicuous

BEST COLOR: No seasonal variation.

AVERAGE LIFE: At least 30 years.

ORIGIN: Unknown

CAUTIONS: None known

SPACING: 10 to 20 feet on center.

Japanese Fern Tree

General: The Japanese Fern Tree is unusual in south Florida. Very little has been written about it in any of the subtropical plant books. I have been watching it for 15 years and have found no problems. The tree is very attractive and easy to grow and maintain. It is a great alternative for Oaks, Mahoganies, and Ficus trees that are commonly planted in areas that are much too small for them.

Companions: The Japanese Fern Tree fits into many different landscape styles. For a manicured look, plant it with Viburnum, Xanadu, and Foxtail Fern. For a tropical look, try combining the Fern Tree with Travelers Palms and Foxtail Palms.

Close-up of the leaf of the Japanese Fern Tree

Care in the Landscape: Japanese Fern Trees are very easy to grow. Fertilize in March, June , and October with a slow-release, well-balanced mix that includes minor elements. If the tree appears shrub-like when young, cut the bottom branches off the trunk. Trim the outer leaves of the canopy to maintain the desired size.

LIGHT: Light shade to full sun. Untested in medium shade.

WATER: After initial establishment period, medium water. Twice a week is ideal. Tolerates irrigation at least up to 3 times a week. Untested without irrigation.

SOIL: Wide range

SALT TOLERANCE: Unknown

WIND TOLERANCE: Unknown

ZONE: 10b to 11. Untested in 10a.

PEST PROBLEMS: None known.

PROPAGATION: Easy to propagate from seeds. I have never tried cuttings.

Botanical Name: *Psidium littorale*

Common Name: **Cattley Guava**

CHARACTERISTICS

PLANT TYPE: Medium tree

AVERAGE SIZE: As a hedge, maintain as low as 5 feet tall by 4 feet wide. As a tree, easily maintained at sizes between 8 feet tall and 6 feet wide and 20 feet tall and 12 feet wide.

GROWTH RATE: Medium

LEAF: Dark, glossy green; about 3 to 4 inches long. New growth is reddish.

FLOWER: Insignificant white flower.

BEST COLOR: Leaf stays the same color all year. Red fruit matures in summer.

AVERAGE LIFE: 30 to 50 years.

ORIGIN: Brazil

CAUTIONS: Do not plant over pavement because fruit is messy.

SPACING: 8 to 15 feet on center.

Easy tree that adapts well to small spots; interesting trunk with peeling bark.

Cattley Guava tree

Cattley Guava bark

General: Cattley Guava is an exceptional tree for south Florida. It is frequently used because of its interesting form, which develops character and multiple trunks as it ages. The bark is quite attractive, a reddish brown color with a textural, peeling quality. This tree is a good substitute for Ligustrum Trees because its leaves stay more attractive, not developing the yellow spots common on Ligustrums. The Guava Tree is not only adaptable to the extremes of the south Florida environment but also adaptable to small spaces. This plant is also used as a hedge, meaning it is very trainable. The Guava fruit is delicious for humans as well as birds, raccoons, and squirrels.

Companions: Cattley Guavas are suitable as medium trees or tall hedges. Good companions include plants with different textures, like Junipers, Wart Ferns, and Zamias. Cocoplum looks good with Guavas because the leaves blend with Guava bark. Silver Buttonwoods are good tree companions because of the contrast of the leaf colors.

Cattley Guava leaves and fruit

Care in the Landscape: To maintain the Cattley Guava as a tall hedge, trim the ends of the branches as needed, normally a few times each year. The trunk is not visible if it is trimmed as a hedge because the branches grow to the ground. The best feature of the Cattley Guava is the trunk, so show it off if the Guava is used as a tree. Remove any small branches that appear on the trunk, so that its interesting form and colorations show. Also, remove any crossed branches in the canopy. Cattley Guavas are not heavy feeders. If you forget to fertilize them, they probably will not notice. They grow in our natural areas with no fertilizer at all. For faster growth, fertilize in March, June, and October with a well-balanced, slow-release mix with minor elements.

GROWING CONDITIONS

LIGHT: Medium shade to full sun.

WATER: After initial establishment period, low water. Ideal is once a week. Tolerates irrigation up to 3 times a week. Survives without irrigation in average environmental conditions.

SOIL: Wide range

SALT TOLERANCE: Low

WIND TOLERANCE: High

ZONE: 9 to 11. Tolerates temperatures at least to 27 deg.F.

PEST PROBLEMS: Fruit flies on the fruit.

PROPAGATION: Seeds, cuttings, or air layers.

Botanical Name: *Ravenala madagascariensis*

Common Name: **Travelers Palm or Travelers Tree**

CHARACTERISTICS

PLANT TYPE: Medium tree

AVERAGE SIZE: Average height is 20 feet. The spread varies from about 15 feet to 30 feet determined by how many trunks are allowed to grow from the base.

GROWTH RATE: Fast. I have seen Travelers Palms grow 4 feet in a month in the summer.

LEAF: Medium green, banana-like; up to 10 feet long by 2 feet wide. The leaf size increases as the plant grows.

FLOWER: Large flower resembles a Bird of Paradise flower but is not as showy because it is green.

BEST COLOR: Flowers in the warmer months, but flower does not add significant color.

AVERAGE LIFE: 30 to 60 years.

ORIGIN: Madagascar

CAUTIONS: None known

SPACING: 8 to 15 feet on center.

A dramatic focal point in a tropical garden. Excellent plant for narrow spots.

Mature Travelers Palm maintained with a single trunk. If untrimmed, Travelers Palms develop multiple trunks, with leaves growing to the ground.

General: The Travelers Palm adds a dramatic focal point without much care. It is not actually a palm, but commonly referred to as such because its trunk resembles one. This unique plant has large, banana-like leaves that grow in a flat plane, resembling a fan. When young (opposite), it closely resembles a White Bird of Paradise. As it matures, its leaves and trunk become larger than a White Bird. The Travelers Palm naturally develops multiple trunks, but it can be maintained with a single trunk, as shown above. The leaves of this plant become split by the wind as it ages.

Companions: The Travelers Palm is an excellent plant for screening along a property line. It also works well along walls, as shown below. The Travelers Palm gives the big-leaf and coarse texture required for the tropical look. Mix it with palms and smaller leaf plants with large flowers, like Hibiscus and Shrimp Plants. It also works beautifully with leaf color, like Ti Plants and Crotons.

A young Travelers Palm

Care in the Landscape: Trim as needed to remove dead leaves and flowers. If a single trunk is desired, trim off suckers (baby plants) from the base. A Travelers Palm is easy to maintain if trimmed at least three times a year. If allowed to go wild, it can be quite a job to get it back within bounds. Fertilize in March, June, and October with a well-balanced, slow-release mix that includes minor elements.

Botanical Name: *Tabebuia caraiba*

Common Name: **Yellow Tabebuia, Yellow Tab**

CHARACTERISTICS

PLANT TYPE: Medium tree

AVERAGE SIZE: 20 to 30 feet tall by 12 to 15 feet wide.

GROWTH RATE: Medium

LEAF: Silvery green, long and pointed; about 3 to 4 inches long by 1 inch wide.

FLOWER: Very showy clusters of yellow flowers. Each flower is about 1 to 2 inches wide and shaped like a bell.

BEST COLOR: Early spring into summer. Blooms on the average for a few weeks a year.

AVERAGE LIFE: At least 50 years.

ORIGIN: Paraguay

CAUTIONS: The tree falls easily and often requires staking, even when mature. The flowers all fall at once, producing slippery surfaces if they fall on pavement.

SPACING: 10 to 20 feet on center.

One of our showiest flowering trees. Lights up south Florida with color every spring.

Yellow Tab in full bloom

General: The Yellow Tab is one of south Florida's most colorful trees. It puts all its bloom energy into a very short time, for a few weeks a year. The tree flowers when it is bare of most of its leaves, with all of the flowers blooming at once. Most other flowering trees have much longer bloom periods but not as high a percentage of color. The Yellow Tab offers the advantage of looking good when it is not blooming. Its form varies from tree to tree but is always interesting and often very unusual.

Companions: Yellow Tabs work well alone, in groups, or with other flowering trees. For great color, mix it with other flowering plants that bloom at the same time. Purple and red Bougainvilleas are the most dramatic companions, particularly if trained as trees. Companion shrubs include Pentas and Crotons.

Close-up of the flower

Care in the Landscape: Yellow Tabs are very easy to grow. They grow almost by themselves, requiring little from us in the way of water, trimming or fertilization. When trees are young, trim off unwanted growth on the trunk. They may fall over in minor winds or if the soil is saturated with water, so stake securely. If fast growth is desired, fertilize in March, June, and October with a well-balanced, slow-release mix that contains minor elements.

GROWING CONDITIONS

LIGHT: Full sun

WATER: After initial establishment period, low water. Ideal is once a week. Tolerates irrigation up to 3 times a week. Survives quite well without irrigation in average environmental conditions.

SOIL: Wide range

SALT TOLERANCE: Medium

WIND TOLERANCE: Low; falls easily when the ground is saturated with water and wind gusts hit the tree.

ZONE: 10a to 11. Survives at least 30 deg.F.

PEST PROBLEMS: None known.

PROPAGATION: Seeds, grafts.

Chapter 6

Large Trees, Over 35 feet tall

Left and above: Our trial gardens are shaded by wonderful native Pine Trees that cool the air in summer and protect the plants from wind and cold in winter. Wildlife enjoy the spot with us.

Botanical Name: *Bauhinia blakeana*

Common Name: **Hong Kong Orchid Tree**

CHARACTERISTICS

PLANT TYPE: Large tree

AVERAGE SIZE: 35 feet tall by 25 feet wide.

GROWTH RATE: Fast

LEAF: Light green, double-sided leaf resembles a cloven hoof; about 3 to 4 inches long by 3 to 4 inches wide.

FLOWER: Large, orchid-like, purple and showy; about 4 inches across.

BEST COLOR: October through April. Blooms for 2 to 3 months during this period.

AVERAGE LIFE: 50 years plus.

ORIGIN: India, Burma, parts of southeast Asia.

CAUTIONS: Weak rooted; leaves and flowers are messy when they drop.

SPACING: 20 to 30 feet on center.

A good winter bloomer that does not leave bothersome or invasive seed pods behind.

Mature Hong Kong Orchid tree

General: The Hong Kong Orchid offers showy color in winter, when most other trees are not flowering. Its bloom period is longer than many flowering trees, sometimes lasting as long as three months. The tree is semi-deciduous, losing many of its leaves when in bloom. Plant the tree so that these fallen leaves will not produce too much of a problem. This fast-growing tree requires little care, provided it has enough room to spread. People frequently plant it in areas that are way too small for its mature size. Many other types of Orchid trees drop ugly seed pods that are not only invasive but also very hard to remove. Not so with the Hong Kong Orchid, which produces no seed pods at all. This is the city tree of Boca Raton.

Companions: For a tropical look, plant the Hong Kong Orchid near a Travelers Palm. It is also a good companion for the Yellow Tab because they sometimes bloom at the same time. The Seminole Pink Hibiscus blends well and usually blooms at the same time as well.

Flowers this beautiful should be hard to grow! Not so for the easy Hong Kong Orchid. The flowers are not only easy but excellent for cutting.

Care in the Landscape: Prune every three to four years to remove crossed branches and dead limbs. This tree does not require much other pruning if it is given enough space to spread naturally. Fertilization is important for the Hong Kong Orchid. Fertilize in March, June, and October with a well-balanced, slow-release mix that contains minor elements. It sometimes shows a potassium deficiency.

NOTES: Hong Kong Orchids frequently defoliate after planting. The chances of defoliation diminish if the tree is planted in the summer.

LIGHT: Light shade to full sun. Blooms best in full sun.

WATER: Low, but tolerates irrigation up to 3 times a week. The Hong Kong Orchid lives happily without irrigation in many areas of south Florida after its initial establishment period.

SOIL: Wide range

SALT TOLERANCE: Low

WIND TOLERANCE: Low

ZONE: 9 to 11. Takes 28 deg. F.

PEST PROBLEMS: Borers

PROPAGATION: Cuttings or air-layering; does not produce seeds.

Botanical Name: *Bursera simaruba*

Common Name: **Gumbo Limbo**

CHARACTERISTICS

PLANT TYPE: Large tree

AVERAGE SIZE: 40 to 50 feet tall by 20 to 40 feet wide.

GROWTH RATE: Medium

LEAF: Bright to deep green; oblong, 3 to 6 inches long by 1 to 3 inches wide.

FLOWER: Greenish white but insignificant, ending as small, dark red fruit that attracts wildlife in winter.

BEST COLOR: No seasonal variation, except for partial defoliation in winter.

AVERAGE LIFE: Over 50 years.

ORIGIN: South Florida and the West Indies.

CAUTIONS: Partially defoliates in the winter.

SPACING: 12 to 30 feet on center.

An excellent native tree with a unique, peeling trunk and a variable form.

Gumbo Limbo with spreading form. Note the difference between this specimen and the one to the right, which is much more upright. The spreading tree above is in a spot where it has space to grow horizontally. The upright tree on the right is in a forest, where it is competing with other trees for vertical space and light. Also, Gumbo Limbo trees grown from branch cuttings grow more horizontally and shorter than those grown from seed. Seed-grown Gumbo Limbos also develop a central trunk or leader more so than those grown from branch cuttings.

General: The Gumbo Limbo is one of south Florida's best native trees. It has two unusual characteristics: no two Gumbo Limbos grow in quite the same shape, and the bark peels off like a sunburned tourist. The tree is semi-deciduous, bare for three or four weeks in the average winter. Branches root easily and are used as living fences around the Caribbean, where termites and rot would quickly ruin most cut fence posts.

Above, left: Gumbo Limbo bark, which peels like a sunburned tourist. Some call it the Tourist Tree. Right: the leaves.

Companions: Other native plants work well with the Gumbo Limbo. Plant it with Pines, Oaks, Mahoganies, Silver Buttonwoods, and Geiger Trees. Sabal Palms, Thatch Palms, and Palmettos also make good palm companions. Some native shrubs that blend well with Gumbo Limbo include Firebush and Cocoplum.

Mature Gumbo Limbo in a natural forest

Care in the Landscape: This tree forms interesting shapes without much pruning. Remove crossed or dead branches from time to time. Gumbo Limbos do not require fertilizer but do grow faster and larger with an occasional application.

Botanical Name: *Delonix regia*

Common Name: **Royal Poinciana**

CHARACTERISTICS

PLANT TYPE: Large tree

AVERAGE HEIGHT: 40 feet tall with a 50 foot spread.

GROWTH RATE: Fast

LEAF: Small, needlelike, about 3/4 inch long. Leaves grow on long stems that give a feathery look.

FLOWER: Color is variable-orange to red. There are also rare yellow and gold blossoms from grafts. Flowers are 3 to 5 inches across and spectacular.

BEST COLOR: Flowers usually appear in May, when the tree is bare, and last until midsummer.

AVERAGE LIFE: At least 50 years.

ORIGIN: Madagascar

CAUTION: If the flowers fall on pavement, it can become slick. Seed pods are large and unattractive. Roots are aggressive; locate at least 25 feet from pavement.

SPACING: 30 to 40 feet on center.

One of the most spectacular flowering trees in the world.

Royal Poinciana Tree

General: The Royal Poinciana is planted and treasured in nearly every frost-free area of the globe. It is truly spectacular. There is even an annual festival in Miami in its honor. Placement of the Poinciana is very important, however, or it can become a problem. Because of its size, plant it in an area that has enough space for it to spread to its 50 foot width. Do not locate too close to pavement. Its root system is quite aggressive and damages pavement, and its flowers make pavement slippery. The tree is quite messy and needs a spot where the droppings and unattractive seed pods will not be too noticeable. Since it is deciduous (bare in winter), plant it among evergreens. An old joke suggests you give one to a neighbor so that you can enjoy it at a distance and not have to deal with its problems. As a specimen tree supplying dramatic color for large locations, it is unequaled.

Companions: To hide the Poinciana's bare winter branches, plant it among evergreen trees, like the Podocarpus, Mahogany, and Japanese Fern Tree. Good shrub companions include Thryallis, Plumbago, Yellow Mussaenda, Cranberry Pentas, and Ruellia Purple Showers. These shrubs bloom at the same time as the Royal Poinciana.

Royal Poinciana flowers

Care in the Landscape: Remove crossed branches and dead wood. Fertilize in March, June, and October with a well-balanced, slow-release mix that contains minor elements.

Royal Poincianas vary somewhat in their form. Notice the shape difference of the above spreading specimen and the more upright one on the opposite page.

GROWING CONDITIONS

LIGHT: Full sun

WATER: Low, but tolerates irrigation up to 3 times a week. Many Poincianas thrive in south Florida without irrigation after their initial establishment period.

SOIL: Wide range

SALT TOLERANCE: Medium

WIND TOLERANCE: Low because the tree is brittle.

ZONE: 10b to 11

PEST PROBLEMS: None serious.

PROPAGATION: Seeds

Botanical Name: *Pinus elliottii*

Common Name: **Slash Pine, Pine Tree**

CHARACTERISTICS

PLANT TYPE: Large tree

AVERAGE SIZE: 50 to 75 feet tall by 20 to 35 feet wide.

GROWTH RATE: Fast

LEAF: Green needles that grow in clusters; 8 to 12 inches long.

FLOWER: Insignificant

BEST COLOR: No seasonal variation.

AVERAGE LIFE: 50 years

ORIGIN: Southeast U.S.

CAUTIONS: A weakened tree is subject to the Pine Borer and inevitable death. Avoid compacting the soil around the roots because it weakens the tree. Plant shrubs and groundcovers at the base of the tree that do not require heavy equipment like lawn mowers to maintain. Do not automatically remove Pines because you think they all die in suburban neighborhoods. Many live happily for many years.

SPACING: Plant staggered sizes close together like they grow in nature, 4 to 12 feet on center.

A great Florida native for creating the high shade that gardens love. Protects the plants underneath from cold and wind.

Mature Slash Pine

General: Slash Pines are the predominant native tree left in south Florida. They are ideal trees for gardeners because the environment they create is ideal for most plants. Their high, loose canopy lets enough sun in for most plants to thrive. The canopy also protects the plants underneath from most of south Florida's cold spells and windy days. The needles that fall acidify our alkaline soils, which most plants love. The needles also form a mulch that is attractive, gives nutrients to the plants, and stays dark brown. The trees cast a light shade that is cooling on hot days.

Companions: To create a native garden, plant Slash Pines with Oaks, Palmettos, and Sabal Palms. Firebush and Cocoplum will provide an appropriate understory for the tree grouping. Or, collect more native shrubs as the years pass to expand the native collection.

The bark of the Slash Pine is attractive not only to humans but also to woodpeckers.

Care in the Landscape: No trimming required. Ideally, the dead branches should be removed but that requires climbing 60 feet up when the tree is mature, so let them fall by themselves. Just be sure you are not standing underneath when they fall. Pine Trees have low nutritional requirements, but some recent studies have shown that overall yellowing of the tree can be due to iron deficiency. If Pines are near a building, sweep the needles off the roof a few times each year. Use the needles as mulch on nearby planting beds. All of our trial gardens are mulched with Pine mulch from the surrounding trees. Leave the areas under the branches planted with anything but grass to avoid having to rake the needles.

GROWING CONDITIONS

LIGHT: Full sun

WATER: Low, but tolerates irrigation up to 3 times a week. Pines live happily throughout south Florida without irrigation after their initial establishment period.

SOIL: Wide range

SALT TOLERANCE: High

WIND TOLERANCE: Medium

ZONE: 8 to 10b

PEST PROBLEMS: Pine Borers.

PROPAGATION: Seeds

NOTE: All of my trial gardens are under Pine Trees (see pages 1,5,6,7,11,166 and 167). I have had less environmental stress on these plants than most gardeners in my area because of the wonderful protection afforded by the trees. The Pines protect my gardens from too much heat, wind, or cold while allowing optimum light. And we have never had to purchase mulch!

Botanical Name: *Podocarpus gracilior*

Common Name: **Podocarpus**

CHARACTERISTICS

PLANT TYPE: Large tree (See also *Podocarpus macrophyllus* on pages 106 and 107 for the shrub Podocarpus.)

AVERAGE SIZE: 50 feet tall by 15 to 30 feet wide.

GROWTH RATE: Medium

LEAF: Dark green; needle like, 2 to 3 inches long.

FLOWER: Insignificant

BEST COLOR: No seasonal variation.

AVERAGE LIFE: At least 50 years.

ORIGIN: East Africa

CAUTIONS: Do not plant over pavement because the tree drops a lot of needles.

SPACING: 15 to 30 feet on center.

A beautiful, under-used tree that lends an evergreen texture to the landscape.

Mature Podocarpus tree with the branches trimmed off the bottom of the trunk. These trees often hold onto their bottom branches naturally.

General: Podocarpus grows as a shrub or a tree. In either situation, it is an excellent plant. The tree is beautiful and well-suited to narrow sites because it can be maintained smaller than most tall trees. It has the look of a northern evergreen. The old leaves of Podocarpus are dark green. The new growth is light green, producing contrast. This tree is a good choice for someone who wants an easy tree that is different from the neighbors. Avoid planting over pavement because it drops a lot of leaves.

Companions: Podocarpus works well with other green textures, like Xanadus, Junipers, Foxtail Ferns, and Zamias. Manicured hedges, like Viburnum, Lakeview Jasmine, and Dwarf Ilex, are also appropriate companions.

Close-up of Podocarpus leaves

Care in the Landscape: Fertilize in March, June, and October with a well-balanced, slow-release mix with minor elements. Trim the tree as needed to maintain desired size and shape. Naturally, the tree develops an interesting shape, like the one on the opposite page. It can also be trimmed into a column. The branches may grow to the ground if not trimmed off. It does not hurt the tree to remove these bottom branches at any time.

Podocarpus can be trimmed into an arch.

Botanical Name: *Quercus laurifolia*

Common Name: **Laurel Oak**

CHARACTERISTICS

PLANT TYPE: Large tree

AVERAGE SIZE: 50 TO 70 feet tall by 30 feet wide.

GROWTH RATE: Fast

LEAF: Deep green and narrow; both sides are shiny. About 1 1/2 inches long by 1/2 inch wide. Leaves are smooth down the sides, which differentiate them from Live Oak leaves, which have serrations down the sides of the older leaves.

FLOWER: Inconspicuous

BEST COLOR: No seasonal variation, except for the fact that the tree is partially bare in the winter.

AVERAGE LIFE: 50 years

ORIGIN: Southeastern U.S.

CAUTIONS: Partially deciduous, meaning it is not as full in the winter, but never completely without leaves.

SPACING: 20 to 50 feet on center.

Faster growing and more upright than the Live Oak, but shorter lived.

Medium-sized Laurel Oak in summer. This tree thins out quite a bit in winter.

General: The Laurel Oak is one of many oaks available in south Florida. It is faster growing but shorter lived than its close relative, the Live Oak. It is also a more upright grower than the Live Oak and has smoother bark. Native to south Florida, its acorns provide food for many birds, squirrels, raccoons, and bears. But, do not worry - bears will not come to your house for the acorns. There are almost no bears left in south Florida. Unfortunately, the tree is not attractive in the small 12 to 15 foot size that is most commonly planted (see photo on opposite page); however, it is an excellent tree and worth some patience.

Companions: Laurel Oaks are excellent street trees, where they look good repeated with about 30 to 40 feet of space between them. In a residential setting, plant a Laurel Oak to provide fast shade and height.

Recently planted Laurel Oak in summer with inset of leaf. This tree is planted a bit to close too the house (See 'NOTE' on page 183).

Care in the Landscape: The Laurel Oak is not a heavy feeder, as it is native to the south Florida soil. However, it grows faster with fertilization in March, June, and October with a well-balanced, slow-release mix with minor elements. The leaves fall from this tree all year, which means they must be raked if grass is underneath. The need for trimming is minimal because the tree is naturally well-formed. It is an excellent choice for replacing Ficus trees, which require frequent pruning and cast shade so deep that plants have a hard time surviving under them. Remove any crossed branches or dead wood every few years.

GROWING CONDITIONS

LIGHT: Light shade to full sun.

WATER: Low, but tolerates irrigation up to 3 times a week. Lives without irrigation in many parts of south Florida after its initial establishment period.

SOIL: Wide range

SALT TOLERANCE: Low

WIND TOLERANCE: Medium

ZONE: 8 to 10b

PEST PROBLEMS: Mushroom root rot; do not overwater.

PROPAGATION: Seeds

Botanical Name: *Quercus virginiana*

Common Name: **Live Oak**

CHARACTERISTICS

PLANT TYPE: Large tree

AVERAGE SIZE: 40 to 50 feet tall by 50 to 60 feet wide.

GROWTH RATE: Medium; grows faster with supplemental water and fertilizer.

LEAF: Dark olive green with a gray cast; about 2 inches long by 1/2 inch wide. Leaves on the new growth have smooth sides. Older leaves show some serrations along the sides. Laurel Oak leaves have smooth sides on all leaves.

FLOWER: Inconspicuous

BEST COLOR: No seasonal variation, except the tree is partially deciduous (fewer leaves in the winter).

AVERAGE LIFE: 100 years

ORIGIN: Southeastern U.S., Central America, Cuba, and Mexico.

CAUTIONS: Partially deciduous, as it is not as full in the winter, but never completely without leaves. Also, damages pavement if planted too close.

SPACING: 30 to 40 feet on center.

One of the best trees in south Florida for attracting wildlife. Easy and beautiful.

The best features of the Live Oak are its spreading canopy and rough bark. Notice how much sunlight shines through the branches.

General: Live Oaks are the most beautiful shade trees in south Florida. Their beauty lies in the spreading, graceful structure of the branches and the rough bark. Many other plants, like Orchids, Resurrection Fern, and Spanish Moss, attach themselves to the trunk, anchored by this rough bark. Mature Live Oaks sometimes look like entire ecosystems, with gardens of natural plants supported by their branches. Many of our south Florida shade trees produce shade too dense for underplantings, and the area underneath becomes sand. Not so for Live Oaks. Their dappled shade is ideal for many of south Florida's lushest foliage. The tree is partially deciduous, not as full in winter as summer. And, it is not particularly attractive when young. But a little patience produces a great reward - a mature Live Oak.

Companions: For a woodland garden, plant masses of Fishtail Ferns and Wart Ferns under an Oak. Add color accents, like Starburst Pentas, Blue Porterflower, Yellow Mussaenda, Walking Iris, Dwarf Powderpuff, and Shrimp. The dappled shade under a Live Oak is ideal for this plant material.

Large Live Oak

Leaf

Medium Live Oak

The lower branches of the large Live Oak have been trimmed to show the house. The medium Live Oak is too small to trim in this fashion.

Care in the Landscape: Live Oaks require little care. They form naturally into good specimens without a lot of pruning. Remove crossed branches and dead wood every few years. Live Oaks do not require fertilizer in average Florida soils. But, if faster growth is desired, fertilize in March, June, and October with a well-balanced, slow-release mix with minor elements. Supplemental water also increases the growth rate of these trees. Live Oaks drop leaves all year. Raking can be a nuisance if grass is planted underneath or the leaves fall on pavement. Oak leaves are one of the best mulches available for the garden.

Note: The spreading character of the Live Oak is well shown on pages 300 and 301.

Botanical Name: *Swietenia mahagoni*

Common Name: **Mahogany Tree**

CHARACTERISTICS

PLANT TYPE: Large tree

AVERAGE SIZE: 35 to 50 feet tall by 30 to 50 feet wide.

GROWTH RATE: Fast

LEAF: New growth is light green. Older growth is dark olive green. Leaves measure about 1 1/2 inches long by 1/2 inch wide.

FLOWER: Insignificant

BEST COLOR: In spring, after the tree partially defoliates, the new growth is bright green.

AVERAGE LIFE: 75 years

ORIGIN: South Florida and the Caribbean.

CAUTIONS: None known

SPACING: 25 to 40 feet on center.

The Mahogany Tree is the easiest shade tree in this book for areas where leaf drop is a maintenance consideration.

Mahogany Tree (see 'NOTES' opposite)

General: The Mahogany is a tough, fast growing shade tree that handles the most difficult of environmental stresses. It thrives in the difficult areas like parking lots, medians, and streets. The Mahogany has the wonderful habit of dropping leaves once a year instead of constantly, like most of our shade trees. This means one big raking a year compared with constant raking required with Oaks or Black Olives if they are planted over grass or pavement. The Mahogany has large, round seed pods that split to release winged seeds. The pods are an attractive mulch, especially in pots. Mahoganies are known for their timber.

Companions: Mahoganies are excellent choices as street trees, when evenly spaced, with about 30 feet in-between. They are also a great choice for residences. For small gardens, one Mahogany will fill the entire garden with shade. It casts a dappled shade that is a little denser than Oak shade but ideal for most of the shade plants in this book.

Close-up of Mahogany leaves

Care in the Landscape: Mahoganies are very easy to grow. The canopy of the tree naturally forms an attractive, rounded shape. Unlike Ficus, the canopy is open enough to avoid the need for constant thinning. Remove any crossed branches and dead wood every few years. The tree is well adapted to our native soils and requires no fertilization. If faster growth is desired, fertilize in March, June, and October with a well-balanced, slow-release mix that contains minor elements. Leaves from the Mahogany fall once a year, making raking an easy chore, as most shade trees drop constantly. It normally takes about two weeks for the leaves to finish falling. Rake them all at once and use them in surrounding beds as mulch. If they start blowing out of the beds, lay some Cypress mulch on top to secure them.

GROWING CONDITIONS

LIGHT: Full sun

WATER: Low, but tolerates irrigation up to 3 times a week. Lives without irrigation in many parts of south Florida after its initial establishment period.

SOIL: Wide range

SALT TOLERANCE: High

WIND TOLERANCE: The tree has a high wind tolerance against uprooting, but the branches are somewhat brittle and break easily.

ZONE: 10b to 11

PEST PROBLEMS: Web-worms frequently eat the leaves in spring, but they grow back quickly.

PROPAGATION: Seeds

NOTES: *The Mahogany Tree in the opposite photo is so close to the drive that it is bound to damage it. All trees this size lift pavement if planted within a few feet. The owner of this home decided to keep the tree because it shaded the cars and house so well. It lifted one portion of the drive a few inches, which was a small price to pay for the shade on hot summer days.*

CHAPTER 7

PALMS

After

Before

The palm is the symbol of the tropics, and very important in the south Florida landscape. However, many are more susceptible to pests and diseases than most other plants in this book. I included 19 palms in this chapter that are some of the easiest available in south Florida today. Two serious problems need to be noted. **Lethal yellowing** is an incurable, serious palm disease that infects many palm species. It wiped out most of the Coconut Palms in south Florida in the 1970's. Subsequently, disease-resistant cultivars were developed, such as the Malayan Dwarf and the Maypan. Some of these newer varieties have developed a susceptibility to the disease years after their introduction. There is always risk with Coconuts. Antibiotic injections help. Before buying a Coconut Palm, check with the nearest County Extension office for the best current cultivars. Other palms are also susceptible, as noted under "PESTS AND DISEASES" for each palm. **Ganoderma** is another serious and incurable disease of older palms. It is a fungus that looks like a mushroom on the trunk of the tree. It enters the trunk through breaks usually caused by weed eaters, or through pruning tools that were used on another tree with ganoderma and not sterilized before using on a different tree. The fungus can persist in the soil for many years. Infected palms must be completely removed and the soil treated. Plant a tree that is not a palm in areas that had palms infected with ganoderma. **Palms included in this book that are least susceptible to either disease include the Bismarckia, Cat Palm, Bamboo Palm, Roebelenii, Lady Palm, Thatch Palm, and Foxtail Palm.**

Pictured (Before, above; After, left): Look at the difference the Palms make to the appearance of the house. From left to right: Foxtail Palm, Alexander Palms on either side of the windows, European Fan Palm in the center of the window, Bismarckia Palm is the silver leaf peeking out, and Royal Palm is the large trunk on the far right. The orange shrub under the window is Acalypha 'Fire Dragon', which we are currently testing.

Botanical Name: *Adonidia merrillii*

Common Name: **Christmas Palm, Adonidia, Dwarf Royal**

CHARACTERISTICS

PLANT TYPE: Palm

AVERAGE SIZE: 15 feet tall by 8 feet wide for single-trunked specimen. Palms with 2 or more trunks are wider.

GROWTH RATE: Medium

LEAF: Medium green; pinnate fronds (shaped like a feather) range from 4 to 5 feet long.

FLOWER: Inconspicuous

BEST COLOR: No seasonal variation.

AVERAGE LIFE: No documented evidence of lifespan. Specimens at Fairchild Tropical Garden have thrived since 1942.

ORIGIN: Philippines

CAUTIONS: High susceptibility to lethal yellowing (see page 185).

SPACING: 6 to 8 feet on center.

One of our most attractive palms, with a useful and unusual small stature.

Triple Dwarf Royal. This plant is not naturally multi-trunked. Three seeds are germinated in one pot to grow triples.

General: The Dwarf Royal is one of our most popular palms for residential use because of its attractive appearance and small size. It is one of the few palms that are commonly available that reaches only fifteen feet in height. Unfortunately, it is highly susceptible to lethal yellowing. (See 'PEST AND DISEASE PROBLEMS', on the opposite page.)

Companions: Dwarf Royals blend with any landscape style. The triple palm on the opposite page is underplanted with an excellent group of low maintenance plants. Ti Red Sisters start the back row, followed by Hibiscus to the right. Sanchezias (the variegated plant) form the next layer. Mammey or Fire Crotons form the next layer, with the Rosy Crown of Thorns as the border.

Before

After

Above (Before): Large, empty expanse of stucco wall appears cold.

Left (After): Dwarf Royal Palms in containers warm up the wall. Notice that small, containerized Dwarf Royals have thin trunks. The trunks thicken up after planting in the ground.

Care in the Landscape: Dwarf Royals are very easy to grow. They are self-cleaning (the old fronds fall off by themselves) and do not need trimming. Though not demanding of nutrition, they benefit from fertilization in March, June, and October with a palm fertilizer.

Botanical Name: *Bismarckia nobilis*

Common Name: **Bismarckia Palm**

CHARACTERISTICS

PLANT TYPE: Palm

AVERAGE SIZE: 30 feet tall by 16 to 20 feet wide.

GROWTH RATE: Slow; medium with fertilization. Growth rate increases after trunk development.

LEAF: Green to gray-blue palmate fronds (shaped like a fan or palm of the hand) are up to 9 feet long.

FLOWER: Insignificant

BEST COLOR: No seasonal variation.

AVERAGE LIFE: No documented study of life-span. Specimens have been thriving at Fairchild Tropical Garden since 1958.

ORIGIN: Madagascar

CAUTIONS: Very difficult to transplant large specimens. Also, be sure to give the Bismarckia at least 16 to 20 feet of space to spread.

SPACING: 20 to 25 feet on center.

One of our finest palm specimens for making a strong statement in the landscape.

A young Bismarckia Palm. The head of the palm develops first to its full 16 to 20 foot width before the trunk starts to show. Since Bismarckias need to be planted small, the biggest mistake made is to underestimate the space they will need when they mature.

General: The Bismarckia Palm is not only distinctive and stately, but also very easy to grow. This large palm with beautiful silver fronds is also resistant to many of the diseases and pests that are plaguing many palm species in south Florida. Given its benefits, one would expect Bismarckias to be more widely used. However, it requires large spaces to accommodate its 20 foot spread. And it is difficult to transplant from a tree farm that grows them in the ground. It is easy to plant from a pot but does not develop much size in a pot. Therefore, enjoying a mature Bismarckia requires patience because it must be planted small. The wait is worth the effort.

Companions: The silver color of the Bismarckia Palm shows best when contrasted with bright colors, like purple or hot pink. Ti Red Sisters or bright red Crotons are spectacular when massed under Bismarckias (see page 75 for a photo of this combination). Purple Queen is a great groundcover for contrast with the silver foliage. Foxtail Palms are also good companions.

(see page 75 for a photo of this combination)

A mature Bismarckia. The spread is about the same as the small one on the opposite page. Age makes the difference in trunk development.

Care in the Landscape: Bismarckias are easy to grow in the landscape. Unlike many palms, they require only moderate fertilization to remain free of nutritional deficiencies. Fertilize in March, June, and October with a palm fertilizer. Trim as needed to remove dead fronds.

GROWING CONDITIONS

LIGHT: Light shade to full sun. The fronds are grayer with more light, fading to green with too much shade. The palm is less compact in shade.

WATER: After initial establishment, low water. Ideal is once a week. Tolerates irrigation at least up to 3 times a week. Untested without irrigation.

SOIL: Wide range

SALT TOLERANCE: Medium

WIND TOLERANCE: High

ZONE: 10a to 11. Survives 32 deg. F. Recovers from minor damage in a season.

PEST AND DISEASE PROBLEMS: None known

PROPAGATION: Seeds

Botanical Name: *Caryota mitis*

Common Name: **Fishtail Palm**

CHARACTERISTICS

PLANT TYPE: Palm

AVERAGE SIZE: 18 feet tall by 8 feet wide.

GROWTH RATE: Medium

LEAF: Dark green leaves emerging from fronds resemble fishtails.

FLOWER: Insignificant

BEST COLOR: No seasonal variation.

AVERAGE LIFE: No documented study of life-span. Specimens have been thriving at Fairchild Tropical Garden since 1936.

ORIGIN: Southeast Asia

CAUTIONS: The seeds are extremely irritating to the skin. This plant is one of the strongest irritants in commonly used landscape plants. It also has roots that are more aggressive than most other palms. Do not plant too close to pavement or in concrete block planters.

SPACING: 6 feet on center for fast-closing mass. 10 feet on center for patient people.

An excellent screening plant for a tropical look. It constantly sends up new shoots from the base, staying quite full.

Fishtail Palms make excellent potted specimens.

General: The Fishtail Palm is an attractive and interesting plant because of its unusual leaves, which resemble fishtails. Use it primarily for screening. It is a nice alternative to the more commonly used Areca Palm. It needs less maintenance than most hedges, but is also taller. Take care not to handle the seeds without gloves, as they are strong skin irritants. Also, do not plant too close to pavement because of the Fishtail Palm's aggressive root system. I once saw it break through a concrete block planter.

Companions: Fishtail Palms are excellent plants for screening. They make an informal hedge if planted six feet on center along a property line. To create a "tropical wall" of screening plants, alternate Fishtail Palms with Travelers Palms and Bismarckia Palms, taking care to leave enough space for the spread of the last two. Keep layering in front with tropical shrubs and groundcovers. Plant contrasting colors or textures directly next to the Fishtails. Other dark green plants with similar textures do not show up.

Mature Fishtail Palm

Care in the Landscape: Fishtail Palms are moderate feeders and appreciate fertilization in March, June, and October with a palm fertilizer. The main care they require is grooming or trimming off the dead fronds. The palm is constantly sending up new shoots from the base. The older fronds die after flowering and require removal to keep the plant attractive.

GROWING CONDITIONS

LIGHT: Dense shade to full sun. Very useful in shade gardens.

WATER: After initial establishment, medium water. Ideal is twice a week in sun or wind or once a week in shade. Tolerates irrigation at least up to 3 times a week. Untested without irrigation.

SOIL: Wide range

SALT TOLERANCE: Low

WIND TOLERANCE: Medium

ZONE: 10b to 11

PEST AND DISEASE PROBLEMS: Moderately susceptible to lethal yellowing (see page 185) and leaf spots caused by fungus.

PROPAGATION: Seeds

Botanical Name: *Chamaedorea cataractarum*

Common Name: **Cat Palm**

One of the few palms that stays small. Easy to grow and a very attractive dark green color.

Cat Palm

The Cat Palm combines well with different textures for a tropical look.

General: The Cat Palm is one of our most useful palms because it is among the few that stay small. Its dark green foliage and full appearance are additional benefits. Its growth habit is shrub-like because it suckers (grows baby plants) from the base. Be sure to give it enough room to spread - at least five feet. Do not confuse the Cat Palm with the Areca Palm. The Areca is more yellow in color and grows much larger.

Companions: Use the Cat Palm as a single specimen, or group three or more as a clump. These useful palms also work well for screening by simply lining them up at five-to-six-foot intervals. Cat Palms are very adaptable to many landscape styles. They work well in formal settings mixed with other dark green textures, like Podocarpus and Lakeview Jasmine. They also work in tropical landscapes when mixed with large leaf textures, like White Bird of Paradise and Philodendron Xanadu.

Cat Palms look good in tropical settings. This palm is surrounded by Ti Plants. A Sago Palm is in front of the Tis. This planting looked great for a few years. Eventually, the Cat Palm spread into the Tis and Sagos, and the planting had to be redone. Cat Palms need a minimum of five to six feet to accommodate their spread. Also, the Sago Palms are falling victim to scale. I currently recommend Cardboard Palm as a substitute.

Care in the Landscape: Cat Palms are very easy to grow. In shade, they require less water and fertilizer than in higher light. They appreciate fertilization in March, June, and October with a palm fertilizer. Trim occasionally to remove dead fronds. This palm is an excellent choice for the low maintenance landscape.

GROWING CONDITIONS

LIGHT: Medium to light shade. An excellent choice for shade gardens. Tolerates more light than the Bamboo Palm (Chamaedorea erumpens) but loses its dark green color in too much sun.

WATER: After initial establishment period, medium. Ideal is twice a week in sun or once a week in shade. Tolerates irrigation at least up to 3 times a week. Untested without irrigation.

SOIL: Wide range

SALT TOLERANCE: Low

WIND TOLERANCE: Unknown

ZONE: 10b to 11

PEST AND DISEASE PROBLEMS: This palm is usually free of pests and diseases in the landscape. Occasional mites or mealybugs are found in nurseries, indoors, or under screening.

PROPAGATION: Seeds

Botanical Name: *Chamaedorea erumpens*

Common Name: **Chamaedorea Palm or Bamboo Palm**

CHARACTERISTICS

PLANT TYPE: Palm

AVERAGE SIZE: 7 to 11 feet tall by 3 to 4 feet wide. This is one of the few palms that can be maintained small, in the 7 foot range.

GROWTH RATE: Medium

LEAF: Dark green pinnate fronds (shaped like a feather) range from about 2 to 3 feet long.

FLOWER: Insignificant

BEST COLOR: Same dark green all year.

AVERAGE LIFE: At least 20 years.

ORIGIN: Mexico

CAUTIONS: Seeds or fruit are irritants.

SPACING: 3 to 4 feet on center.

One of the few plants available that features a thin, vertical growth habit and thrives in deep shade.

The recently planted Bamboo Palm is the tallest plant in the corner. Ti Red Sisters and a Peppermint Ti are directly in front, followed by a Sago Palm. Snowbush shrubs form the tallest layer on either side of the Bamboo Palm, with Caricature plants in front. Watermelon Peperomia forms the border. (Note: I had high hopes for Watermelon Peperomia for the first three years I used it. Then, it developed major problems with snails and fungus.)

General: The primary benefits of the Bamboo Palm are small size and adaptability to very low light. Used as a popular house plant for decades, this palm thrives with less light than most. Its growth habit is similar to an Areca Palm, but it stays much smaller and greener. The Bamboo Palm is taller and thinner than its relative, the Cat Palm.

Companions: Use the Bamboo Palm as a specimen to accent a shady corner or any space that needs something tall and thin. I have found it extremely useful in bath atriums, in-between windows, and under screening. Most palms planted under screening will eventually hit the top, but not the Bamboo Palm. Use it with bright colors, like the Ti Red Sister, or light colored plants, like Sanchezia. In deep shade, use the Bamboo Palm with other plants that are also popular for indoor use, like Corn Plants and Pothos.

Older Bamboo Palm

Care in the Landscape: Bamboo Palms are very easy to grow. In deep shade, they need little fertilization or water other than rain. In more light, they appreciate fertilization in March, June, and October with a palm fertilizer. If a branch dies or becomes too tall, trim it at the ground. New, shorter shoots grow continually from the base.

Botanical Name: *Cocos nucifera*

Common Name: **Coconut Palm**

CHARACTERISTICS

PLANT TYPE: Palm

AVERAGE SIZE: 30 to 80 feet tall by 15 to 30 feet wide, depending on cultivar.

GROWTH RATE: Medium

LEAF: Green pinnate fronds (shaped like a feather) range from 8 to 15 feet long. Stalks vary in color, from green to yellow, depending on cultivar.

FLOWER: Insignificant

BEST COLOR: No seasonal variation.

AVERAGE LIFE: No documented study of life-span. Specimens have been thriving at Fairchild Tropical Garden since 1964.

ORIGIN: Throughout the tropics.

CAUTIONS: Expect falling coconuts. Susceptible to lethal yellowing (see 'PEST AND DISEASES PROBLEMS', opposite).

SPACING: 10 to 20 feet on center.

PROPAGATION: Seeds (coconuts).

Symbol of the tropics and the relaxing life-style of the sea.

A clump of Coconuts at Fairchild Tropical Garden in Miami

General: The Coconut Palm is native to many of the world's most famous beaches. It is symbolic of the relaxed life-style of these areas. The sound the fronds make when they catch a breeze is a wonderful addition to a tropical garden. The Coconut Palm is also one of our toughest palms, withstanding harsh salt and wind conditions right up to the shoreline. It is extremely easy to grow but susceptible to lethal yellowing (see 'PESTS AND DISEASE PROBLEMS' on the opposite page).

Companions: For a tropical look, mix Coconuts with Travelers Palms, Japanese Fern Trees, and Silver Buttonwood Trees (if you are near salt water). These large, tropical trees form a great background for the next layer of Crotons, Sanchezias, Tis and Shrimp Plants. Border with Wart Ferns or Ruellia Katies, depending on light conditions.

Coconut Palms at the beach. The shape of the trunks varies from straight to curved. Coconuts are also pictured on pages 274, 275, and 297.

Care in the Landscape: Coconut Palms grow on the beaches of south Florida without any fertilizer, irrigation, or trimming. Obviously, they are tough. They adapt well to a landscape situation, handling more water, if necessary. For faster growth or to prevent a possible potassium deficiency, fertilize in March, June, and October with a palm fertilizer. Old fronds fall off by themselves. Remove the coconuts if they pose a threat.

GROWING CONDITIONS

LIGHT: Full sun

WATER: After initial establishment period, low water. Ideal is once a week. Tolerates irrigation up to 4 times a week. Survives without irrigation.

SOIL: Wide range

SALT TOLERANCE: High

WIND TOLERANCE: High, except for the Malayan Dwarf, which snapped at the ground in many cases at Fairchild Tropical Garden in Miami during Hurricane Andrew.

ZONE: 10b to 11.

PEST AND DISEASE PROBLEMS: Coconut mite, palm aphids, ganoderma, bud rot, and lethal yellowing. Lethal yellowing is an incurable, serious palm disease that wiped out most of the Coconut Palms in south Florida in the 1970's. Subsequently, disease-resistant cultivars were developed, such as the Malayan Dwarf and the Maypan. Some of these newer varieties have developed a susceptibility to the disease years after their introduction. There is always risk with Coconuts. Antibiotic injections help. Before buying a Coconut Palm, check with the nearest County Extension office for the best current cultivars. See page 185 for more information on ganoderma.

Botanical Name: *Dypsis decaryi*

Common Name: **Triangle Palm**

CHARACTERISTICS

PLANT TYPE: Palm

AVERAGE SIZE: 25 feet tall by 12 to 16 feet wide.

GROWTH RATE: Medium

LEAF: Grayish-green pinnate fronds (shaped like a feather) range from about 6 to 10 feet long.

FLOWER: Insignificant

BEST COLOR: No seasonal variation.

AVERAGE LIFE: No documented study of life-span. Specimens have been thriving at Fairchild Tropical Garden since 1947.

ORIGIN: Madagascar

CAUTIONS: None

SPACING: 12 to 16 feet on center.

A low maintenance palm with a unique, geometric appearance.

A young Triangle Palm. The head develops to its full size before the trunk develops. Curly Ruffles surround the palm. Red Pentas and Lantana are planted in front.

General: The Triangle Palm makes a dramatic statement in any landscape. The trunk is arranged in three flat sides, like a triangle. Use it alone or in groups. If room allows, group three together for strong impact.

Companions: For a tropical look, plant Triangle Palms with Travelers Palms or White Birds of Paradise. For lower layers, mix with shrubs and groundcovers that either have a contrasting texture, like Curly Ruffles and Philodendron Xanadus, or bright colors. Some bright shrub companions include Ti Red Sisters, Crotons, Firespikes, Cranberry Pentas and Shrimp Plants. Groundcover suggestions include Purple Queens, Ground Orchids, and Bromeliads.

The trunk is emerging on this more mature Triangle Palm.

Care in the Landscape: Fertilize in March, June, and October with a palm fertilizer. Remove fronds when they are brown. Add extra manganese if leaves appear frizzled. Triangle Palms are also susceptible to potassium deficiency.

Botanical Name: *Dypsis lutescens*

Common Name: **Areca Palm**

CHARACTERISTICS

PLANT TYPE: Palm

AVERAGE SIZE: 20 feet tall by 8 feet wide.

GROWTH RATE: Medium

LEAF: Greenish-yellow pinnate fronds (shaped like a feather) range from about 2 to 6 feet long. Yellow leaf stems.

FLOWER: Inconspicuous

BEST COLOR: No seasonal variation.

AVERAGE LIFE: No documented study of life-span. Specimens have been thriving at Fairchild Tropical Garden since 1955.

ORIGIN: Madagascar

CAUTIONS: Not a palm for a manicured, low maintenance look. This plant requires frequent grooming to look neat and orderly. A good choice for a natural garden.

SPACING: 6 to 10 feet on center.

An inexpensive palm that gives a tropical look. Great source of fast screening.

An Areca Palm trimmed so that the individual trunks show

General: Areca Palms are not the favorite of palm enthusiasts, probably because they are so common. Through the years, I have come to terms with their usefulness. For inexpensive screening, they cannot be duplicated. They will block out an unattractive view in the day it takes to plant them. Arecas are a good choice for those who want a natural look, not for those who want a perfect, dark green palm without any brown fronds. The natural color of the leaf stems is yellow. For a low maintenance palm, expect some brown fronds.

Companions: Areca Palms are primarily massed together in the landscape to form a large hedge. These palms are also attractive when mixed with other large tropicals to provide more interest. Travelers Palms and White Birds of Paradise make good partners. For companion plantings, Arecas look best with bright colored plants, like Ti Plants and Crotons.

Areca Palm growing naturally. See page 241 for another Areca Palm.

Care in the Landscape: Fertilize in March, June, and October with a palm fertilizer. Arecas show nutritional deficiencies primarily by yellow foliage. Their stems are yellow naturally. To trim an Areca like the one on the left, remove the small growth at the base to uncover the large trunks. New growth will continually appear at the base, so this can be a high maintenance task. Arecas like the one above are much easier to maintain. The small growth at the base is allowed to grow to achieve a more shrub-like appearance. Trim off old, dead fronds.

See page 241 for another Areca Palm.

GROWING CONDITIONS

LIGHT: Dense shade to full sun. One of the most adaptable plants in this book to varying light conditions. Much thinner in deep shade.

WATER: After initial establishment period, low water. Ideal is once a week in sun or wind, once every other week in shade. Tolerates irrigation at least up to 3 times a week. Survives without irrigation in average environmental conditions.

SOIL: Wide range

SALT TOLERANCE: Medium

WIND TOLERANCE: Low

ZONE: 10b to 11. An Areca Palm in my backyard in Boca Raton died in one of the freezes in the early 80's.

PEST AND DISEASE PROBLEMS: Relatively pest free in the average south Florida garden. I have seen occasional cases of ganoderma (see page 185). In a nursery, indoors, or under screening, watch out for caterpillars, mealybugs, and scale.

PROPAGATION: Seeds

Botanical Name: *Livistona chinensis*

Common Name: **Chinese Fan Palm**

CHARACTERISTICS

PLANT TYPE: Palm

AVERAGE SIZE: 30 feet tall by 8 to 10 feet wide.

GROWTH RATE: Slow

LEAF: Medium green palmate fronds (shaped like a fan or palm of the hand) range from 3 to 6 feet across.

FLOWER: Insignificant

BEST COLOR: No seasonal variation.

AVERAGE LIFE: No documented study of life-span. Specimens have been thriving at Fairchild Tropical Garden since 1956.

ORIGIN: China

CAUTIONS: Sharp thorns on stalks.

SPACING: 8 to 10 feet on center.

An easy, slow growing palm that is frequently misused as a groundcover.

A mature Chinese Fan Palm

General: The Chinese Fan Palm is an attractive palm that is very easy to grow. Its slow growth makes it more expensive than the more common Queen Palms or Washingtonia Palms. Chinese Fan Palms are attractive when quite young, which has led to the common mistake of planting them as a groundcover. Those who do so have difficulty believing that the palm will grow to 30 feet and cannot be kept smaller with pruning.

Companions: The Chinese Fan Palm has coarse, palmate leaves. Palmate leaves are shaped like a hand, with fingers extended. They contrast well with the finer, pinnate leaves (tiny leaflets growing from a common stem) of Queen Palms and Roebeleniis. The Chinese Fan Palm also blends well with large-leaf shrubs, like Crotons and Ti Plants.

A medium-sized Chinese Fan Palm

Care in the Landscape: Fertilize in March, June, and October with a palm fertilizer. Chinese Fan Palms do not show nutritional deficiencies as readily as Queens or Roebeleniis. The old fronds fall off by themselves, making this a very, easy-care palm.

A small Chinese Fan Palm planted as a groundcover. It will outgrow the spot quickly and have to be removed.

GROWING CONDITIONS

LIGHT: Medium shade to full sun.

WATER: After initial establishment period, low water. Ideal is once a week in sun or wind, once every other week in shade. Tolerates irrigation at least up to 3 times a week. Survives without irrigation in average environmental conditions.

SOIL: Wide range

SALT TOLERANCE: Medium

WIND TOLERANCE: High

ZONE: 10a to 11

PEST AND DISEASE PROBLEMS: Medium susceptibility to lethal yellowing and ganoderma. See page 185 for more information.

PROPAGATION: Seeds

Botanical Name: *Phoenix roebelenii*

Common Name: **Pygmy Date Palm or Roebelenii**

CHARACTERISTICS

PLANT TYPE: Palm

AVERAGE SIZE: 10 feet tall by 6 feet wide.

GROWTH RATE: Slow

LEAF: Medium green, pinnate fronds (shaped like a feather) range from about 3 to 5 feet long.

FLOWER: Inconspicuous

BEST COLOR: No seasonal variation.

AVERAGE LIFE: No documented study of life-span. Specimens have been thriving at Fairchild Tropical Garden since 1940.

ORIGIN: Southeast Asia

CAUTIONS: Beware of sharp spines on fronds.

SPACING: 4 to 6 feet on center.

Used throughout south Florida for decades. One of the few palms that stays relatively small.

A single Roebelenii

General: The Roebelenii is one of the most commonly used palms in south Florida. It is one of the few palms that stays reasonably small, which makes it a valuable asset to south Florida residences. The Roebelenii is easy to grow and extremely wind-resistant. It withstood Hurricane Andrew better than any other palm in south Florida. The palm naturally grows with a single trunk but is more commonly grown with double or triple trunks. These multiple trunks occur when multiple seeds are planted in the same pot.

Companions: The Roebelenii works well in many landscape styles. In a manicured garden, combine it with Philodendron Xanadus and Crown of Thorns (photo on page 102). For a tropical look, mix with Ti Plants, Crotons, and Shrimp Plants. The Roebelenii even works well with Pentas and Plumbago in a cottage garden.

Right (Before): A bare new house

Below (After): A triple Roebelenii. This plant is not naturally multi-trunked. Three seeds were germinated in the same pot to grow this palm. Roebeleniis are commonly available with one, two, or three trunks. Four to seven trunks are available but more difficult to find.

Before

After

Care in the Landscape: Trim the dead fronds off the bottom but be careful with the thorns. Fertilize in March, June, and October with a palm fertilizer. Be sure the fertilizer includes magnesium, manganese, and potassium because this palm sometimes shows deficiencies of these elements. If the fronds appear frizzled, apply extra manganese.

Botanical Name: *Ptychosperma elegans*

Common Name: **Alexander Palm or Solitaire Palm**

Attractive, easy palm that fits well into small spaces.

Triple Alexander Palm. This palm does not naturally grow with multiple trunks. Three seeds are germinated in a pot to get this effect. Double Alexander Palms are shown on pages 121 and 264.

General: The Alexander Palm is an excellent choice for the low maintenance landscape. It is attractive, relatively inexpensive, and easy to grow. One of the few commonly available palms that is appropriate for small areas, it is especially useful in courtyards and atriums where space is tight. But, remember its ultimate height of 20 feet. It cannot be maintained lower. I have seen many people plant it under pool screening, not realizing that it would eventually have to be removed.

Companions: Whatever the landscape style, this palm will fit. For a tropical look, combine it with the White Bird of Paradise, Seminole Pink Hibiscus, Ti Plant, Croton, and Shrub Allamanda. For a cottage look, mix with the Anderson Crepe Hibiscus, Dwarf Powderpuff, Blue Porterflower and Thryallis.

Three small Alexander Palms are planted close together, as they should be. Ti Red Sisters are in the middle of the palms, followed by Shrub Allamanda. Aztec Grass or Variegated Liriope forms the border.

Care in the Landscape: Fertilize in March, June, and October with a palm fertilizer. The dead fronds fall off by themselves. This is an extremely easy plant.

Botanical Name: *Ptychosperma macarthurii*

Common Name: **Macarthur Palm**

CHARACTERISTICS

PLANT TYPE: Palm

AVERAGE SIZE: 25 feet tall by 6 to 10 feet wide.

GROWTH RATE: Medium

LEAF: Bright green, pinnate fronds (shaped like a feather) range from 4 to 7 feet long. The ends of the leaflets are notched.

FLOWER: Inconspicuous

BEST COLOR: No seasonal variation.

AVERAGE LIFE: No documented study of life-span. Specimen thriving at Fairchild Tropical Garden since 1938.

ORIGIN: New Guinea

CAUTIONS: Seed is an irritant.

SPACING: 5 to 10 feet on center.

PROPAGATION: Seeds

A multi-trunked palm that is much easier to maintain than the more common Areca Palm.

Macarthur Palm neatly trimmed into a few trunks

General: The Macarthur Palm is an excellent choice because of its attractive appearance and ease of maintenance. It looks similar to an Alexander Palm. The Alexander naturally has a single trunk; however, the Macarthur has multiple trunks that constantly grow from the base. They can be removed to produce a neatly trimmed palm with a few trunks or allowed to grow naturally into a mass of fronds. The Macarthur is a good substitute for the more common Areca Palm because it does not yellow as easily or require as much trimming.

Companions: Planted in groups, Macarthur Palms form an effective privacy screen. For more diversity, use Travelers Palms, White Birds of Paradise, Japanese Fern Trees, and Anderson Crepe Hibiscus with the Macarthur Palms to form a tropical screen.

Macarthur Palm in a more natural state

Care in the Landscape: Fertilize in March, June, and October with a palm fertilizer. For a palm clump, not much trimming is required. The old fronds fall off by themselves. For defined trunks, selectively prune off the small growth to uncover the main trunks. Subsequently, trim off the new growth at the base.

GROWING CONDITIONS

LIGHT: Medium shade to full sun.

WATER: After initial establishment period, low water. Ideal is once a week in sun or wind, once every other week in shade. Tolerates irrigation at least up to 3 times a week. Survives without irrigation in average environmental conditions.

SOIL: Wide range

SALT TOLERANCE: Medium

WIND TOLERANCE: Low

ZONE: 10b to 11. Survives 32 deg. F. but shows damage to the leaves at about 38 deg.F.

PEST AND DISEASE PROBLEMS: Scale and mites indoors or under screening. Ganoderma (page 185) is a threat in the landscape. Some spots are always on the leaves but are not worth treating unless the condition becomes severe.

PROPAGATION: Seeds

Botanical Name: *Rhapis excelsa*

Common Name: **Lady Palm**

CHARACTERISTICS

PLANT TYPE: Palm

AVERAGE SIZE: 6 to 8 feet tall by 5 to 6 feet wide.

GROWTH RATE: Slow

LEAF: Dark, glossy green palmate fronds (shaped like the palm of a hand) range from about 1 to 2 feet long.

FLOWER: Inconspicuous

BEST COLOR: No seasonal variation.

AVERAGE LIFE: No documented study of life-span. Specimens have been thriving at Fairchild Tropical Garden since 1973.

ORIGIN: East Asia

CAUTIONS: Yellowing is a sign of an iron deficiency.

SPACING: 4 to 6 feet on center.

Unique appearance, small size, and ease of care make this a useful palm.

Lady Palms are good choices for pots.

General: The Lady Palm has been successfully used in the south Florida landscape for decades. With its shrub-like growth habit, it seldom grows taller than eight feet. Popular as an indoor plant, the Lady Palm thrives in low light. It is useful in pots or planted in the ground. Use it as a single specimen or group several as a mass. Groups of Lady Palms make beautiful, but expensive hedges.

Companions: For an informal, tropical look, mix Lady Palms with large-leaf plants, like White Bird of Paradise and Philodendron Xanadu. The dark green color of the palm contrasts well with variegated plants, like Sanchezia or Variegated Arboricola. For color, combine with bright-colored plants, like Ti Plants and Crotons.

Mix the Lady Palm with other textures for a tropical look.

The Lady Palm is a good choice under pool screening because it does not outgrow the space.

GROWING CONDITIONS

LIGHT: Dense to light shade. Leaves turn yellow in too much light.

WATER: After initial establishment period, medium water. Ideal is once a week in deep shade, twice a week in bright light or wind. Tolerates water at least up to 4 times a week. Untested without irrigation.

SOIL: Wide range

SALT TOLERANCE: Medium

WIND TOLERANCE: High

ZONE: 9 to 11

PEST PROBLEMS: Scale and mealybugs.

PROPAGATION: Seeds or division of suckers.

Care in the Landscape: Fertilize in March, June, and October with a palm fertilizer. For iron deficiency (shown by yellow leaves, if the plant is in shade), use a fertilizer with at least 2% iron content. Trim to remove brown fronds. This palm puts out suckers, or baby plants, at the base. Remove them as desired.

Botanical Name: *Roystonea elata*

Common Name: **Royal Palm**

CHARACTERISTICS

PLANT TYPE: Palm

AVERAGE SIZE: 60 to 90 feet tall by 20 feet wide.

GROWTH RATE: Medium

LEAF: Medium, lime green pinnate fronds (shaped like a feather) range from about 8 to 10 feet long.

FLOWER: Insignificant

BEST COLOR: No seasonal variation.

AVERAGE LIFE: No documented study of life-span. Specimens have been thriving at Fairchild Tropical Garden since 1955.

ORIGIN: South Florida

CAUTIONS: Heavy, mature fronds can cause damage to whatever happens to be underneath when they fall. Also, seeds (fruits) are an irritant.

SPACING: 12 to 30 feet on center.

One of the most beautiful of Florida's native palms. Large-scale and stately.

Mature Royal Palms lining a street in a formal arrangement

General: The regal stature and large scale of this palm are the reasons for the name, Royal Palm. With its trunk resembling a concrete pillar, the Royal Palm has an architectural look. This palm is self-cleaning, which means that its fronds fall off by themselves without trimming. This feature, along with its adaptability to native soils, results in a palm that is very easy to maintain.

Companions: Royal Palms are traditionally used in south Florida for formal street plantings. Use these regal palms also for informal tropical gardens. Mix with other palm textures, such as Roebeleniis and Foxtail Palms. Understand the mature height of Royals before planting them.

Right (Before): The roots from the Ficus Tree were damaging the driveway.

Below (After): Royal Palms replace the Ficus for a whole new look. The red-flowered shrubs beneath the palms are Jatrophas. A Sago Palm and Foxtail Ferns are planted in front.

Before

After

Care in the Landscape: The Royal Palm is native to cypress swamps and similar areas of south Florida with richer soils than those found in many Florida residences. Regular fertilizations are necessary in poor, sandy soil. Fertilize in March, June, and October with a palm fertilizer. Royal Palms are especially susceptible to manganese and potassium deficiencies. Manganese deficiency is characterized by frizzled new leaves that are yellow, weak, and smaller than the rest. Add extra manganese sulfate, or the palm may die. Potassium deficiency affects the oldest leaves first, with yellow or orange specks appearing on the leaves. Add potassium if this occurs.

Botanical Name: *Sabal palmetto*

Common Name: **Sabal Palm or Cabbage Palm**

CHARACTERISTICS

PLANT TYPE: Palm

AVERAGE SIZE: 40 feet tall by 8 to 10 feet wide.

GROWTH RATE: Slow

LEAF: Gray-green palmate fronds (shaped like a fan or palm of the hand) range from 3 to 8 feet long.

FLOWER: Insignificant

BEST COLOR: No seasonal variation.

AVERAGE LIFE: No documented study of life-span. Specimens have been thriving at Fairchild Tropical Garden since 1966.

ORIGIN: Southeastern United States.

CAUTIONS: None

SPACING: 5 to 10 feet on center.

The state tree. Native to all of Florida. Still plentiful in the wild.

Young Sabal Palms have "boots" (old leaf bases) that form the texture on this trunk. Sabal Palms are also shown on pages 123 and 303.

General: The Sabal Palm is native to Florida and still plentiful in the wild. It is the state tree. Most of the ones now planted in landscapes are harvested from the wild. This palm is protected by law, however, and harvesting should be restricted to areas that are being cleared for development. If the palms are too young to have trunks, they cannot be transplanted. When transplanting, chances of survival increase if fronds are removed.

Companions: Sabal Palms are informal and work well in loose clusters of staggered heights. They blend well with other natives, such as Cocoplums, Oaks, Pines, and Palmettos.

Right: A Sabal Palm's chances of survival with transplanting are greatly increased if most of the fronds are removed. The fronds grow back as the palm establishes itself in the landscape.

Sabal Palms shed their "boots" from their trunks as they age. Note the smooth trunk on this older palm compared to the rough trunk of the younger palm on the opposite page.

Care in the Landscape: This palm is technically self-cleaning, but the fronds persist on the tree longer than some people like. Trim as needed. Sabal palms thrive in our native soils even without fertilizer, although their appearance improves if fertilized in March, June, and October with a palm fertilizer.

Botanical Name: *Serenoa repens*

Common Name: **Saw Palmetto**

CHARACTERISTICS

PLANT: Palm

AVERAGE SIZE: 6 to 8 feet tall by 6 to 10 feet wide.

GROWTH RATE: Slow

LEAF: Light green to silvery green, palmate fronds (shaped like a fan or palm of the hand) range from about 2 to 6 feet long.

FLOWER: Inconspicuous

BEST COLOR: No seasonal variation.

AVERAGE LIFE: No documented study of life-span. Specimens have been thriving at Fairchild Tropical Garden since 1939.

ORIGIN: Florida and the southeastern coast of the U.S.

CAUTIONS: The name Saw Palmetto comes from the thorns on sides of the stalks that make the stalk resemble a saw.

SPACING: 3 to 6 feet on center.

A hardy Florida native with a sculptural look when mature. Great plant in a garden to attract wildlife.

A clump of Palmettos planted closely as a groundcover. Eventually, they grow as large as the one opposite.

General: Saw Palmettos are extremely hardy plants growing naturally in our pinelands. If they occur naturally on a site, preserve them, not only because they are quite valuable financially, but also because they provide valuable habitat for wildlife. I was once called to a home that the owner had recently purchased, where there were quite a lot of Palmettos. He thought they were weeds and asked for a price for their removal. I estimated the value of the group at $50,000. The owner changed his mind about removal and has developed quite a liking for his Palmettos. They protect the bases of pine trees from too much heavy traffic. The old Palmettos develop very interesting trunk shapes that can form the focal point of the landscape. Saw Palmettos are infrequently planted in new landscapes because they are difficult to move when large and very slow to develop if planted small.

Companions: I love to use Palmettos in gardens designed to attract wildlife. Pines, Oaks and Sabal Palms are natural tree companions. Most birds and butterflies like diversity in their foods, just like people. Few people like the same meal every night. Use many different shrubs and groundcovers with Palmettos to attract a lot of wildlife. Cocoplum, Thryallis, Firebush, Jatropha, Firespike, Shrimp Plant, Pentas, Plumbago, Ruellia, Blue Porter-flower and Golden Senna are some suggestions.

Above, left: A small green Palmetto. Above, right: A small silver Palmetto. Below: A clump of Silver Palmettos with the undergrowth trimmed off to reveal the sculptural trunks.

Care in the Landscape: Palmettos are one of the easiest plants in this book. They adapt to many different environmental extremes - high or low water, sun, light shade, high winds, and/or poor soil. For a naturalistic look, Palmettos require very little care. For a manicured look, they require trimming of dead fronds several times each year. Palmettos have very low nutritional needs and seldom need fertilizer.

Botanical Name: *Syagrus romanzoffiana*

Common Name: Queen Palm

CHARACTERISTICS

PLANT TYPE: Palm

AVERAGE SIZE: 30 to 40 feet tall by 10 to 12 feet wide.

GROWTH RATE: Fast

LEAF: Dark green pinnate fronds (shaped like a feather) range from 5 to 10 feet long.

FLOWER: Insignificant

BEST COLOR: No seasonal variation.

AVERAGE LIFE: No documented study of life-span. Specimens have been thriving at Fairchild Tropical Garden since 1971.

ORIGIN: Brazil and Argentina.

CAUTIONS: Expensive to hire a tree trimming company to trim after it grows too big to reach the fronds with a pole pruner or ladder. Fruit can be messy after it falls.

SPACING: 8 to 20 feet on center.

One of the most commonly used palms in south Florida. Graceful and easy to grow.

Mature Queen Palm

General: The Queen Palm is the most common palm in south Florida because it transplants well and grows quickly and easily. The best feature of the appearance of the palm is its gracefulness, which contrasts well with coarser-textured palms, like Royals and Xmas Palms. The trunk is rougher than many other palms, particularly when the Queen Palm is young.

Companions: Queen Palms work well in groups. For an informal grouping, use odd numbers of palms in staggered heights, with at least a three foot difference in height of each palm. For example: place three palms in one group, one at 12 feet, one at 15 feet, and one at 18 feet tall. For a more formal appearance, line up palms of the same size equidistant from each other (photo pages 284 and 285).

This 12 foot Queen Palm has been planted in this garden for about six weeks. It was transplanted from a tree farm and lost its bottom fronds, which is normal after transplanting. The head fills out again fairly quickly.

Care in the Landscape: Old fronds on Queen Palms do not fall off by themselves until they are quite unsightly. Trim them off as needed. This is easy when the palm is short enough to reach the frond with a pole pruner or ladder. When the palm is too tall, you may need help from a tree company, which can be expensive. Fertilize in March, June, and October with a palm fertilizer. Susceptible to manganese and potassium deficiencies.

GROWING CONDITIONS

LIGHT: Light shade to full sun.

WATER: After initial establishment period, low water. Ideal is once a week in sun or wind, once every other week in shade. Tolerates irrigation at least up to 6 times a week. Survives without irrigation in average environmental conditions.

SOIL: Fairly adaptable except in extremely alkaline soils.

SALT TOLERANCE: Medium

WIND TOLERANCE: Low

ZONE: 10a to 11. Into central Florida.

PEST PROBLEMS AND DISEASE PROBLEMS: Ganoderma (page 185), bud rot.

PROPAGATION: Seeds

NOTE: Also susceptible to "frizzletop", a deficiency of manganese, especially on alkaline soils. Most palm fertilizers include extra manganese. If the palm is fertilized regularly and still exhibits frizzled fronds, apply extra manganese.

Botanical Name: *Thrinax radiata*

Common Name: **Thatch Palm or Florida Thatch Palm**

CHARACTERISTICS

PLANT TYPE: Palm

AVERAGE SIZE: 20 feet tall by 6 wide.

GROWTH RATE: Slow

LEAF: Bright green, palmate fronds (shaped like a fan or palm of the hand) range from 3 to 5 feet long. Yellowish ribs.

FLOWER: Insignificant

BEST COLOR: No seasonal variation.

AVERAGE LIFE: No documented study of life-span. Specimens have been thriving at Fairchild Tropical Garden since 1939.

ORIGIN: South Florida and the Caribbean.

CAUTIONS: None known

SPACING: 6 to 10 feet on center.

An excellent Florida native. Its small size and ease of care make this a valuable asset in a small garden.

Mature Thatch Palm in the landscape

General: Thatch Palms are smaller in stature than most of the commonly used palms. Only extremely old ones reach their full height of 20 feet. This unusually small size makes them a valuable asset to a small-scaled garden. Thatch Palms are not only easy to grow but very tolerant of salt and drought. They are also resistent to many of the diseases and pests that are plaguing many palm species. Native to south Florida, their existence is currently threatened in the wild.

Companions: The palmate shape of the Thatch Palm (similar to a hand) contrasts well with pinnate palms (feather shaped) like Roebeleniis, Queen Palms, and Royal Palms. For a tropical look, mix Thatch Palms with large leafed plants, like Travelers Palms and White Birds of Paradise.

Right: The roofs of Tiki huts were frequently woven of Thatch Palm fronds by the Seminole Indians.

Below: A young Thatch Palm in a nursery.

Care in the Landscape: Thatch Palms are very easy to grow. They are remarkably resistant to palm pests and diseases. Since they are well adapted to our native soils, they generally do not require fertilizer. To increase its slow growth rate, fertilize in March, June, and October with a palm fertilizer. Trim off old fronds if they become unsightly.

PALMS 221

GROWING CONDITIONS

LIGHT: Medium shade to full sun. Best form in full sun.

WATER: After initial establishment period, low water. Ideal is once a week in sun or wind, once every other week in shade. Tolerates irrigation at least up to 3 times a week. Survives without irrigation in average environmental conditions.

SOIL: Wide range

SALT TOLERANCE: High

WIND TOLERANCE: High

ZONE: 10b to 11

PEST AND DISEASE PROBLEMS: None known

PROPAGATION: Seeds

Botanical Name: *Wodyetia bifurcata*

Common Name: **Foxtail Palm**

CHARACTERISTICS

PLANT TYPE: Palm

AVERAGE SIZE: 30 feet tall by 10 to 14 feet wide.

GROWTH RATE: Fast

LEAF: Dark green pinnate fronds (shaped like a feather) range from about 5 to 7 feet long.

FLOWER: Insignificant

BEST COLOR: No seasonal variation.

AVERAGE LIFE: Unknown. This palm was introduced into south Florida in 1983.

ORIGIN: Australia

CAUTIONS: None known

SPACING: 6 to 15 feet on center.

Attractive trunk, unique fronds, and ease of care make this a great palm.

A Foxtail Palm with Ground Orchids behind it

General: The Foxtail Palm is a wonderful addition to the commonly available palms in south Florida. It is smaller than Royal and Queen Palms, which makes it ideal for most residences. The trunk and crown shaft are smooth, like a royal Palm, which most people find very attractive. The most distinctive characteristic of the Foxtail is the texture of the fronds, which resemble foxes' tails. This palm is also remarkably free of most common palm pests and diseases and extremely easy to grow.

Companions: Use the Foxtail Palm alone as a specimen or in groups. It adapts well to informal groupings of staggered heights or more formal avenue plantings. The interesting leaf texture adds diversity to a palm garden, including finer-textured Roebeleniis and coarser-textured Coconut Palms. The pinnate fronds (shaped like a feather) contrast well with palmate fronds (shaped like a fan or palm of the hand), like those of the Thrinax Palms.

A group of three Foxtail Palms surrounded by Red Pentas and Yellow Crossandra.

Care in the Landscape: Foxtail Palms are very easy to grow. No trimming is required because the palm is self-cleaning (the old fronds fall off by themselves.) Fertilize in March, June, and October with a palm fertilizer.

GROWING CONDITIONS

LIGHT: Light shade to full sun.

WATER: After initial establishment, medium water. Ideal is twice a week in sun or wind or once a week in shade. Tolerates irrigation at least up to 3 times a week. Untested without irrigation.

SOIL: Wide range

SALT TOLERANCE: Medium

WIND TOLERANCE: Medium

ZONE: 10a to 11. Most experts expect damage at 32 deg. F., but many Foxtail Palms seem to have survived the 1989 freeze (25 F.).

PEST AND DISEASE PROBLEMS: No known pests; leaf spots and fungus appear occasionally.

PROPAGATION: Seeds

CHAPTER 8

EASY LOW WATER GARDENS

After

Before

WATER-SAVING PRACTICES

- CREATE SHADE
- LIMIT AREAS OF GRASS
- WATER EFFICIENTLY
- MANAGE YOUR GRASS CORRECTLY

Above (Before): South Florida's most common landscape style includes hedges and grass that require frequent trimming. In addition, grass requires much more water than most landscape shrubs.

Left (After): A new landscape that requires much less maintenance and water. The plant with yellow and green leaves is Variegated Arboricola. The border plants are Dwarf Crown of Thorns. Mammey Crotons form the middle layer. Cranberry Pentas bloom at the base of the fountain. This combination requires trimming about twice a year as compared with the grass above, which needs cutting about 35 times per year! The new garden requires watering, at most, once a week and provides constant color for years.

TIME FOR A NEW APPROACH

It is time for a new approach - we need a way of creating beauty in our landscape without wasting water, harming our environment, or ruining our backs with maintenance.

There is a common misconception that flowers require a lot of water. While Impatiens do, most of the flowering plants in this book actually do better with less water. The yellow Shrimp Plants and Cranberry Pentas above do best with water once or twice a week. The border is Torenia, an annual with higher water demands. Ruellia Katie is a perennial groundcover that would give the purple color without the increased water needs.

For generations, south Florida has been blessed with an abundant water supply - as much as we could possibly want for landscape irrigation. Because of this abundance, we were never concerned about how much we watered. Overwatering results in shorter life-spans, more disease, more maintenance and increases the need for fertilizer. With rapid population growth and a simultaneous loss of wetlands to store our water, we are now facing water restrictions every few years in south Florida.

Plants need half as much water in shade than in full sun. This principle is so important to low water, low maintenance landscapes that I devoted a whole chapter to shade (pages 238 to 257). The garden below shows the beauty that is possible with low water, low maintenance gardens in shade. Pink Angelwing Begonias are the tallest pink flowers. Shrimp Plants bloom in the middle, with purple Ruellia Katie in front. (The Ruellia gets more light than the Angelwing Begonias.) A Mend Bromeliad accents the rock.

LIMIT AREAS OF GRASS

Grass requires more water, maintenance, and fertilizer than any other area of the landscape. It makes sense to limit its use to cut down on water and maintenance requirements. Grass is the only groundcover we have that takes foot traffic. It is useful in play areas or places where people congregate. Creative ideas for replacing grass are explored throughout this book.

Before

Left (Before): A boring backyard that requires water at least twice a week to keep it green. The Black Olive tree was dropping brown tannic acid in the pool.

Right (After): Grass is replaced with shrubs and groundcovers that require one half to one third as much water. A Queen Palm and Travelers Palm replace the Black Olive. Stepping stones provide a surface for walking. Ti Red Sisters form two color accent groups and contrast well with the variegated leaves of the Sanchezia. The Peperomia groundcover was eaten by snails and is not recommended. Notice how the plants are kept back from the screening. The view from a screened area is unattractive if leaves are mashed up against the screen. Also, the garden is designed to be viewed from inside the screening, with the lowest layers closest to the screen and graduating up from there.

After

LIMIT AREAS OF GRASS

Left (Before): A side yard where most people plant grass. This home-owner wanted a more attractive view from the rooms which overlook this side.

Before

Right (After): The new garden not only looks much better than just grass, but it also uses one half to one third the water. Two different colors of gravel form the structure of the design, which are separated by aluminum edging. The low water landscape should have separate sprinkler zones for the grass and the rock area, since the grass needs so much more water.

Tips for using gravel as groundcover: Use small stones for good coverage.

The gravel needs to be at least two stones deep so use stones 3/4" or smaller. If larger stones are used, they are too large to be placed two stones deep, and the spaces in-between show dirt and allow more weeds to grow. If you prefer the look of larger stones, put two inches of small gravel as a base and sprinkle the larger stones on top. Weeds grow through concrete here so expect them to appear in your gravel, whatever size you use. See the maintenance chapter to learn how to minimize weeds (page 316). Do not use gravel in areas of poor air circulation because it mildews. Also, avoid gravel in areas where leaves will fall on it.

After

Water Efficiently

Overwatering is the gravest error gardeners commit in Florida. This common practice shortens a plant's life, causes disease, and increases the maintenance requirements of each plant. The plant grows faster with more water and, therefore, needs more trimming. The growth is often leggy because the plant is frantically trying to figure out where to store all this water; thus, long, loppy stems result. Overwatered plants also require more fertilizer than properly watered plants because the water washes the fertilizer through the soil.

Overwatering stresses our environment when we have droughts. In severe droughts, water is diverted from wildlife areas to satisfy plants that do not really need it. It is time for a change.

There is no plant in this book that requires more water than twice a week after its initial establishment period. Most of the plants in this book prefer watering once a week. Many survive with no supplemental irrigation at all.

Establishment Watering

Recently-planted shrubs, trees and groundcovers need frequent, deep watering to establish their roots in the ground. The watering schedule depends upon the plants' environment. Shade gardens require half the water of sun gardens. Windy gardens require more water than calm gardens. Plants require twice as much water in summer heat than in winter cool. If it sounds confusing, remember that your plants will tell you when they need water by wilting.

Once I had a call from a customer who told me that his recently planted landscape was dying. I went to his house and saw a garden dying of thirst. He told me it couldn't be thirst because it had rained that morning. It had sprinkled just a little. Imagine that you are very thirsty, and someone gives you a thimble filled with water. It is not enough, and you remain thirsty. *Newly planted material needs enough water to soak the entire root ball with each application.* It takes about one inch of water to soak the soil to a depth of one foot. Put several empty coffee cans in your garden and see how long your sprinklers need to run to fill them to a depth of one inch. Every time you run your sprinklers, apply one inch of water. Watering to this depth gives adequate water to most plants that were grown in containers in a nursery.

Field-grown trees present another problem. These are trees that were grown in the ground in a tree farm. Their roots are cut so that they can be transplanted into your landscape. They require more water than containerized plants because their root balls are bigger (often two to three feet in depth), and they have been through the trauma of having their roots cut. One easy way to do this is to have different sprinkler heads installed at the base of each tree. Adjustable flood bubblers are ideal. They flood the base of the tree, giving much more water to it than to the surrounding plants. The adjustable feature allows you to cut down on the water by tightening a screw, so the water is diminished as the tree becomes established.

Another great alternative for establishment watering is a soaker hose. The water comes slowly out of the sides of a soaker hose, seeping down to the roots of a plant. These low-volume hoses are ideal for establishment watering because the slow soaking gives the roots time to absorb the water. Quick, high-pressure water sometimes goes by a plant's roots so fast that the roots do not have a chance to absorb the water. Soaker hoses can be placed either under or on top of the mulch.

Soaker hose

Soaker hoses are ideal for establishing field-grown trees. Wrap them around tops of the root balls (on top of the ground) in a circle at the bases of the trees. Palms normally lose their lower fronds during establishment, but I have seen them retain all their leaves with soaker hoses. These low-volume hoses are also ideal for beds of shrubs and groundcovers. They do not work well for grass. *At the time of the publication of this book, soaker hoses are exempt from all water restrictions, making it easily possible to plant during the most severe water restrictions.*

Soaker hoses require much more time to apply one inch of water than conventional sprinklers. For trees, plan on using the soaker hoses for six months. Let them run all night for the first three weeks, turning them off in the daytime. Cut down to five nights a week during the fourth week, four times a week during the fifth through eighth week, and three times a week during the next two months. Cut down to twice a week for the next two months. Obviously, turn them off when it rains enough to give the root balls a good soaking.

For shrubs and groundcovers, plan on using the soaker hoses for a minimum of four hours at each application. Watch the plants carefully for signs of wilt, and then turn the hoses on again. The establishment period is about six months for shrubs and groundcovers, but they will not require anywhere near as much water as field-grown trees. The schedule for establishment watering of shrubs and groundcovers varies tremendously, based on temperature, wind, and sunlight. The following schedule is an estimate for either soaker hoses or traditional sprinklers:

First month - every day
Second month - every other day
Third month through sixth month - twice a week

Remember that the plants need twice as much water on 95 degree days than they do on 80 degree days. If plants are planted in July and there is no rain for a week, they may require twice as much water or twice a day for the first month. If they are planted in shade in December, they may only need one half the water stated above. This schedule assumes one inch of water per application. Purchase a rain gauge so you can measure your rainfall. If it rains one inch or more, do not water that day.

The number one reason for plant death in the landscape is lack of water during the establishment period. In most instances, the cause is not lack of turning on the water but a clogged sprinkler head. If a piece of sand gets into a head, it can clog it, and the water will not hit part of the area the head should cover. If you experience plant wilt on one plant but not on the same type of plant that is next to it, turn on your sprinklers and see if both are receiving equal water. Another way to test a system easily is to put out multiple coffee cans, run the system at night, and then see how much water is in each can the next morning.

WATER THE ESTABLISHED LANDSCAPE

After diligently watering during the establishment period, many find it hard to understand that, for shrubs, trees, and ground-covers, the need for water greatly diminishes after the first six months in the ground. Overwatering after establishment is a frequent cause of plant problems. After the roots of the plant have grown, the roots not only give the plant a place to store more water, they also grow deep into the ground to pick up water you do not see on the surface. The grass becomes the major water user.

The establishment period water is weaned off over a period of time. This weaning encourages the roots of the plant to grow deeper to find water. If the roots are large and healthy, the leaves and flowers follow suit. Plants properly weaned off water are much more able to withstand drought conditions than plants that are habitually overwatered. Overwatered plants do not develop sufficient root systems that will allow them to go for a long time without more water.

I have seen many instances of daily watering of plants that have been in the ground for years! Their roots have never grown down more than a few inches to reach for water. Overwatered plants are nutritionally deficient because water causes their nutrients to wash quickly through the soil. They are leggy and gangly because the overwatering causes extra fast growth. They are often full of pests because plants in a weakened state attract pests. Fungus is a frequent disease problem. Their life-spans are greatly diminished.

The plants in this book are tolerant of differing water conditions, which is very important. The cornerstone of the low water, low maintenance landscape is its ability to adapt to our environment. The south Florida climate is normally dry in winter and very wet in summer. If desert plants are planted when we have a drought, they may not be able to take the next tropical storm that drops twelve inches of water on the garden in a single day. But, even the most tolerant plants cannot handle daily water for years on end.

Using adaptable plants keeps both the design process and the sprinkler system easy because the plants can all be watered on the same schedule. The grass needs more water than any of the shrubs, so it makes sense to put it in a separate sprinkler zone, if possible.

Be sure to water at night or early in the morning. Watering at noon can use twice as much water than watering at four in the morning because of evaporation.

The amount of water your plants require varies, based on the type of plant and the type of soil. It is also greatly affected by the amount of sun, wind, and heat. Because of the differing environmental conditions, it is impossible to give weekly watering requirements for all plants. On the individual plant pages of this book, I have put down estimates for each plant. Use these estimates as just that - estimates. Watch your plants and see how much water they need in your landscape. After six months in the ground, few plants in this book need water more than once a week, unless they are in fine sand, high wind, and bright sun all at the same time! Signs of water stress include wilting or having the bottom leaves of a plant yellow and fall off. We often get more than one inch of water a week, so use nature for plant water when it's available, and use sprinklers only when it is very dry.

Keep your sprinklers well maintained. They require checking at least monthly. Turn the system on and run it through all its zones. If a head is broken, a geyser can result, which is a huge water user. Check each area to see that it is getting 100% coverage.

WATER THE ESTABLISHED LANDSCAPE

The shrubs and trees in this garden only need water about once a week after establishment. The grass needs water about twice a week. Although the plants tolerate twice a week watering, it makes sense to put the grass on a separate sprinkler zone. The trees with pink flowers are Anderson Crepe Hibiscus. Petra Crotons have the orange and yellow leaves in the background. Ixora Nora Grant is the shrub with the pink flowers, bordered by Aztec Grass. Ti Red Sisters have the dark red leaves, with Purple Queen in front.

MANAGE GRASS CORRECTLY

Grass is the biggest water user in the south Florida landscape. If possible, keep it on separate sprinkler zones from your shrubs, trees, and groundcovers. Then, you can water it more than the rest. Most people who have this system find they seldom water their shrub and tree areas.

Given our situation of more frequent water restrictions, it makes sense to condition your grass for drought. Grass that is not conditioned will not withstand a drought very well. The same principles that apply to shrub watering apply to grass: water deeper and less often to produce a healthy root system. Frequent, light waterings are the worst thing you can do to your grass.

Do not water your lawn until you see it needs water. Signs that a lawn needs water include: footprints remain long after being made, leaf blades have folded in half lengthwise, and bluish-grey spots appear in the lawn. Apply 3/4 inch of water. Do not water again until you see the same signs. Expect it to take up to six weeks to condition your grass to go for more than a few days without showing signs that it needs water. In time, it will go for longer periods because it is growing a larger root system. You will receive the added benefit of a better looking, thicker, greener lawn through this process.

Mowing grass higher not only toughens it against drought but also increases its general health. Use the highest setting for your mower blade. Keeping mower blades sharp also increases the drought tolerance. And, do not cut too much at once; remove no more than one third of the height with each cut.

Maintain your Sprinklers

Broken sprinklers are a major cause of excess water use. Check your sprinklers monthly. A missing or broken head becomes a geyser, as shown on the left. A head turned the wrong way waters the pavement instead of the grass (below). If sprinklers are not routinely checked, this water waste can go on for years.

EXAMPLES OF LOW WATER FLOWER GARDENS

A popular misconception is that flower gardens require a lot of water. The garden to the right requires water no more than once a week in average environmental conditions once it is established. Plumbago is growing up an arch behind the bench. Yellow Mussaenda has the white and yellow flowers. Ti Red Sisters are directly behind the bench. Shrimp Plants have the yellow flowers on either side of the bench. Red Spot Crotons are in the green pots.

The garden to the right has no automatic sprinkler system. This is one of our trial gardens. We hand water this garden so that we can closely monitor its water use. Only the pots need water more than once or twice a week.

CHAPTER 9

EASY SHADE GARDENS

After

Before

- ASSESSING SHADE

- DENSE SHADE PLANTS AND GARDENS

- MEDIUM SHADE PLANTS AND GARDENS

- LIGHT SHADE PLANTS AND GARDENS

- MIXED LIGHT PLANTS AND GARDENS

Shade is one of our most valuable tools for adapting to the south Florida environment. Trees cool the temperatures and provide cover for wildlife. Shade gardens use only one half to one third as much water as sun gardens. Trees protect the plants from wind and cold damage. All of our trial gardens are in light shade. People are amazed at how good the plants look after wind storms or cold snaps.

Above and left (Before and After): The front of the house is transformed with easy shade color. Angelwing Begonias are the tallest pink flowers, surrounded by yellow Shrimp Plants. Caricature Plants provide the dark leaves under the windows. Wart Ferns form the border, with Fire Crotons between the Shrimps and the Wart Ferns. This combination offers year-round color in shade with very little care.

ASSESSING SHADE

The most difficult challenge I meet is assessing the degree of shade in a garden. If the sun stayed in the same place all the time, it would be easy. But it moves from east to west every day and from north to south every year.

I have developed a simple method, which works most of the time. Get a compass and go to the spot. Pretend you are the plant. Put yourself in your garden in the location you are considering for the plant. Put your eye at the level of the plant and look around. Look up, down, as well as 360 degrees around. Since the sun moves throughout the day, do this mid-morning, at noon, and mid-afternoon. This observation gives you a good understanding of the amount of light the plant would receive at different times of the day.

Understand that the angle of the sun moves. At noon in June, the sun is straight overhead. At noon in December, it is further south. Imagine this change as you observe the sun. The seasonal difference can be significant for plants. Some locations are full sun in summer and medium shade in winter. If these locations have plants that burn in sun, the landscape will burn up during its first summer.

DENSE SHADE: Look up and you will see the dense shade of Ficus, Bischofia, or Black Olive trees or the roof of a building. Less than 30% of the sky is visible. Look down and see almost nothing growing, not even weeds. Look all around and see little sky, only more dense trees or buildings.

MEDIUM SHADE: Look up and you will see medium shade from Oaks, Mahoganys, Palms, or Pines. Look for about 50% or more of sky. Look down and see ferns or other shade plants growing. St. Augustine grass is thin at best, as it needs more sun to grow. Look around and see more trees but not much open sky on the south or west sides. Sun from the south or west is strong and too much for most medium shade plants.

LIGHT SHADE: Look up and you will see about 20%-30% leaves and the rest sky. The trees are planted farther apart in light shade than in medium shade. Look down and notice many types of plants growing, including St. Augustine grass. Look around and see many patches of sky from any direction.

MIXED LIGHT: These areas get both direct sun and full shade and are normally found near buildings. The change in light is due to the movement of the sun, either from morning to evening or from winter to summer. If the movement is from winter to summer, it can be difficult to assess without a compass. Be sure to picture the seasonal sun movement when assessing the light. Plants in mixed light need the ability to adapt to extremes.

Areca Palms form the shade to cool the Pink Angelwing Begonias, yellow Shrimp Plants, and flowering Bromeliads in the pots. This garden is an example of medium shade. Colored pots are a great accent for any garden.

DENSE SHADE PLANTS

Under 1'

Pothos

1'-3'

Liriope   Variegated Arboricola   Fishtail Fern   Walking Iris   Wart Fern

Anthurium Lady Jane   Cast Iron Plant

2.5'-4'

Variegated Arboricola   Walking Iris   Snake Plant

4'-6'

Lady Palm   Variegated Arboricola   Corn Plant

6'-8'

Variegated Arboricola   Lady Palm   Dracaena marginata   Corn Plant   Bamboo Palm

8'-15'

Lady Palm   Dracaena marginata

15'-35'

Fishtail Palm   Kentia Palm   Areca Palm

TIPS FOR PLANTING IN DENSE SHADE

• Understand that dense shade is very limiting. Not many plants grow in so little light. The majority of the plants on the opposite page are most commonly used as house plants.

• Keep it simple. Do not try to use plants that need more light, like the plants recommended for medium shade. They will not perform well. I commonly see Ti Plants and Crotons planted in dense shade. They go into a slow decline and look bad after a few months. Use Tis and Crotons in medium shade to sun situations.

• Use garden accessories if you want more interest. Accessories do not need light to thrive, and you have many more options for design impact.

The owners of this dense shade bath atrium had tried medium shade plants, like Tis and Crotons, to create an attractive view. They did not work because the area did not have enough light to support them. I replaced them with a simple French lattice, a pot on a pedestal, and two very low light plants: Pothos on the lattice and Lady Jane Anthuriums in the pot. The accessories do not need light and make the design statement in this garden.

PLANTS TO AVOID

Some house plants that have not worked well in the landscape in south Florida include Aglaonema, Marantas, Calatheas, and Dieffenbachias. They like warmer climates and have consistently shown severe leaf damage in our winters. Anthuriums die in rather cold years. They all died in the winter of 1995 as far south as Boca Raton. I included them in the table (opposite) because of their unique ability to flower in dense shade. Other than cold sensitivity, they are easy plants. Spathiphyllums, or Peace Lilies, do beautifully some years but eventually get eaten by snails.

MEDIUM SHADE PLANTS

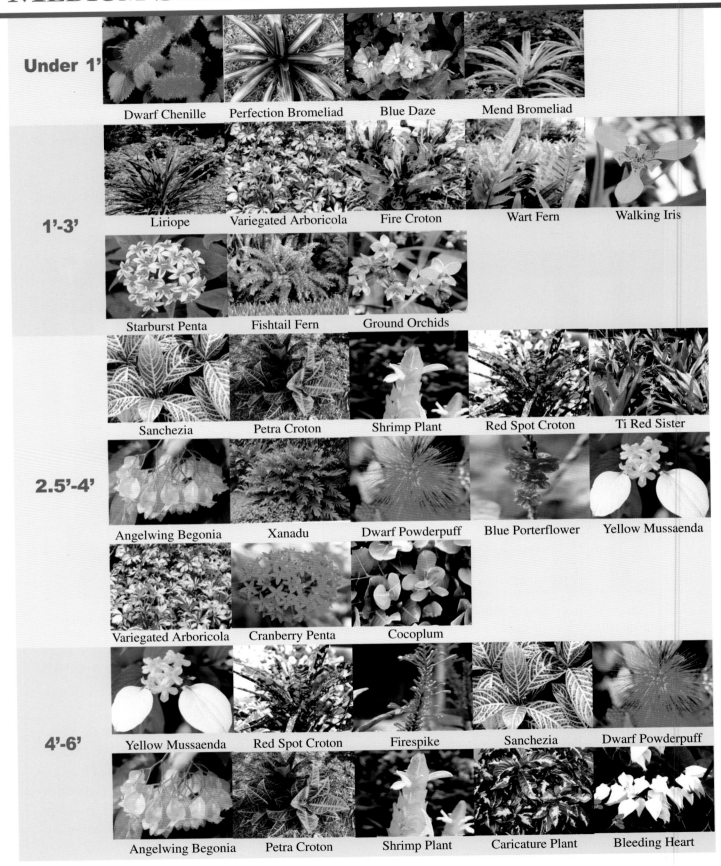

Under 1'

Dwarf Chenille · Perfection Bromeliad · Blue Daze · Mend Bromeliad

1'-3'

Liriope · Variegated Arboricola · Fire Croton · Wart Fern · Walking Iris

Starburst Penta · Fishtail Fern · Ground Orchids

Sanchezia · Petra Croton · Shrimp Plant · Red Spot Croton · Ti Red Sister

2.5'-4'

Angelwing Begonia · Xanadu · Dwarf Powderpuff · Blue Porterflower · Yellow Mussaenda

Variegated Arboricola · Cranberry Penta · Cocoplum

4'-6'

Yellow Mussaenda · Red Spot Croton · Firespike · Sanchezia · Dwarf Powderpuff

Angelwing Begonia · Petra Croton · Shrimp Plant · Caricature Plant · Bleeding Heart

4'-6'

Zamia | Variegated Arboricola | Viburnum | Ti Red Sister | Cocoplum

6'-8'

Starburst | Sanchezia | Lady Palm | Angelwing Begonia | Bamboo Palm

Cat Palm | Cocoplum | Caricature Plant | Variegated Arboricola | Viburnum

8'-15'

Cattley Guava | White Bird | Starburst | Xmas Palm | Bamboo Palm

Roebelenii | Cocoplum

15'-35'

Fishtail Palm | Alexander Palm | Areca Palm | Macarthur Palm | Thatch Palm

Travelers Palm | Chinese Fan Palm

35'+

Mahogany Tree | Live Oak | Laurel Oak

MEDIUM SHADE GARDENS

Left (Before): The medium shade in this garden does not provide enough light to support the Juniper groundcover.

Before

Right (After): Medium shade plants replace the old plantings. These homeowners love color, especially from leaves. Their breakfast room overlooks this garden, so the space is important to them. The light green of the large Australian Tree Fern contrasts well with the Ti Red Sisters directly behind the fern. Petra Crotons form the next layer, with Variegated Peperomia (which was later eaten by snails) and Perfection Bromeliads as groundcover. Shrimps peek out on the bottom left.

After

LIGHT SHADE PLANTS

Under 1'

Blue Daze · Purple Queen · Dwarf Chenille · Ruellia Katie

Liriope · Fire Croton · Foxtail Fern · Spider Lily · Ilex

Dwarf Ixora · Fishtail Fern · Starburst Pentas · Wart Fern · Ground Orchid

1'-3'

Walking Iris · Dwarf Fak. Grass · Variegated Arboricola · Cocoplum · Lakeview Jasmine

Cranberry Pentas · Viburnum

Cocoplum · Ilex · Dwarf Ixora · Shrub Allamanda · Dwarf Powderpuff

2.5'-4'

Petra Croton · Thryallis · Red Spot Croton · Ti Red Sister · Caricature Plant

Firebush · Ixora Nora Grant · Jatropha · Lakeview Jasmine · Ixora Super King

2.5'-4'

Viburnum • Xanadu • Plumbago • Podocarpus • Ruellia Purple Showers

Variegated Arboricola • Blue Porterflower • Shrimp Plant • Sanchezia • Pinwheel Jasmine

4'-6'

Cat Palm • Shrub Allamanda • Cocoplum • Dwarf Powderpuff • Blue Butterfly

Jatropha • Petra Croton • Yellow Mussaenda • Caricature Plant • Firebush

Red Spot Croton • Shrimp Plant • Ti Red Sister • Lakeview Jasmine • Firespike

Ixora Super King • Plumbago • Podocarpus • Ruellia Purple Showers • Sanchezia

Variegated Arboricola • Pinwheel Jasmine • Viburnum • Zamia • Bleeding Heart

6'-8'

Bamboo Palm • Cat Palm • Roebelenii • Lady Palm • Palmetto

6-8'

Sanchezia — Seminole Pink Hibiscus — Caricature Plant — Ixora Nora Grant — Cocoplum

Starburst — Viburnum — Lakeview Jasmine — Firebush — Podocarpus

Ixora Super King — Petrea Vine — Jatropha — Confederate Jasmine — Variegated Arboricola

8'-15'

Bamboo Palm — Cocoplum — Cattley Guava — White Bird — Starburst

Jatropha — Roebelenii Palm — Lakeview Jasmine — Anderson Crepe Hibiscus — Senna surattensis

Seminole Pink Hibiscus — Golden Senna — Xmas Palm

15'-35

Fishtail Palm — Areca Palm — Chinese Fan Palm — Alexander Palm — Macarthur Palm

Thatch Palm — Travelers Palm — Cattley Guava — Triangle Palm — Palmetto

15'-35'
Foxtail Palm   Podocarpus   Japanese Fern Tree

35'+
Mahogany Tree   Live Oak   Laurel Oak   Bismarckia Palm   Sabal Palm

Queen Palm

Medium Shade versus Light Shade

The difference between medium shade and light shade is sometimes difficult to determine. Medium shade means more shade than sun, and light shade means more sun than shade. The plants suggested for medium shade might burn in a light shade situation. Angelwing Begonias, for example, are suggested for medium shade but not light shade because their leaves will burn if exposed to too much sun. None of the plants suggested for light shade will burn, so if you are concerned about too much sun for shade plants, choose the plants suggested for light shade.

LIGHT SHADE GARDENS

This garden receives morning sun filtered through screening and afternoon shade. Screening provides light shade for plants. The palm in the corner is a Roebelenii. Fishtail Ferns drape over the spa. Ti Red Sisters provide an excellent contrast, with their dark red leaves next to the lime green of the ferns. Shrimp plants provide the yellow flowers.

Before

Left (Before): The light shade in this garden is ideal for most of the plants in this book.

Right (After): Cranberry and White Pentas combine with yellow Shrimp Plants to complement this native garden.

After

MIXED LIGHT PLANTS

Under 1'

Dwarf Chenille Blue Daze

1'-3'

Liriope Variegated Arboricola Fire Croton Cocoplum Cranberry Pentas

Starburst Pentas Viburnum

Cranberry Pentas Petra Croton Shrimp Plant Viburnum Ti Red Sister

2.5'-4'

Pinwheel Jasmine Xanadu Dwarf Powderpuff Blue Porterflower Yellow Mussaenda

Variegated Arboricola Red Spot Croton Cocoplum

4'-6'

Yellow Mussaenda Viburnum Firespike Cat Palm Dwarf Powderpuff

Ti Red Sister Petra Croton Shrimp Plant Red Spot Croton Pinwheel Jasmine

4'-6'

Zamia   Cocoplum   Variegated Arboricola

6'-8'

Viburnum   Starburst   Roebelenii Palm   Cocoplum   Cat Palm

Variegated Arboricola

8'-15'

Cattley Guava   White Bird   Starburst   Xmas Palm   Cocoplum

Roebelenii

15'-35'

Fishtail Palm   Alexander Palm   Areca Palm   Macarthur Palm   Thatch Palm

Travelers Palm   Chinese Fan Palm   Cattley Guava

35'+

Mahogany Tree   Live Oak   Laurel Oak

MIXED LIGHT GARDENS

This page: This garden flows through both sun and shade. The same plants thrive in both light conditions. Ti Plants, Shrimps, Cranberry Pentas and Variegated Arboricolas are excellent choices for this difficult environment.

Opposite: White Birds, Tis, Crotons, and Aztec grass work well by this pool, with its morning shade and afternoon sun.

Tips for Gardening in Mixed Light

Some gardens have extremes of light, with one part medium shade and another bright sun. Other gardens are in shifting light, with hot sun in summer and medium shade in winter. The plants on the previous pages fit well into these gardens. All of them adapt to different light conditions, from medium shade to bright sun. They also adapt to full sun all day or medium to light shade all day. They differ from the plants categorized as 'Light Shade' because they tolerate more shade. Many of the 'Light Shade' plants would not be happy in a 'winter shade, summer sun' situation because they would go for months with only medium shade. Plants, like Ixora Nora Grant, need more light than this.

CHAPTER **10**

EASY SUN GARDENS

After

Before

- **PLANTS FOR SUN**

- **GARDENS FOR SUN**

Above (Before): House in need of landscape renovation

Left (After): Relandscaping gives the house a complete facelift. It looks like the house itself has been completely renovated instead of just the plantings. This house faces south and gets sun all day. The plants love the heat, thriving in this difficult environment. Alexander Palms are underplanted with a clump of Ti Red Sisters. Shrub Allamandas, with their yellow flowers, are bordered with Aztec Grass. Corkscrew Crotons line the porch.

FULL SUN PLANTS

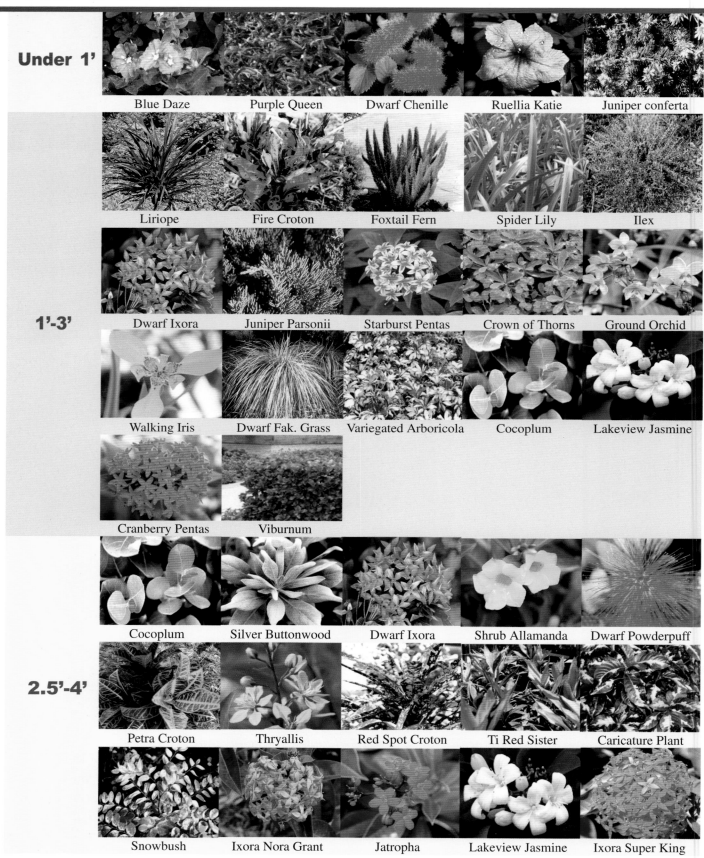

Under 1'

Blue Daze · Purple Queen · Dwarf Chenille · Ruellia Katie · Juniper conferta

1'-3'

Liriope · Fire Croton · Foxtail Fern · Spider Lily · Ilex

Dwarf Ixora · Juniper Parsonii · Starburst Pentas · Crown of Thorns · Ground Orchid

Walking Iris · Dwarf Fak. Grass · Variegated Arboricola · Cocoplum · Lakeview Jasmine

Cranberry Pentas · Viburnum

2.5'-4'

Cocoplum · Silver Buttonwood · Dwarf Ixora · Shrub Allamanda · Dwarf Powderpuff

Petra Croton · Thryallis · Red Spot Croton · Ti Red Sister · Caricature Plant

Snowbush · Ixora Nora Grant · Jatropha · Lakeview Jasmine · Ixora Super King

2.5'-4'

Viburnum — Xanadu — Plumbago — Podocarpus — Ruellia Purple Showers

Variegated Arboricola — Blue Porterflower — Shrimp Plant — Sanchezia — Pinwheel Jasmine

Cat Palm — Shrub Allamanda — Cocoplum — Dwarf Powderpuff — Blue Butterfly

Jatropha — Petra Croton — Yellow Mussaenda — Caricature Plant — Firebush

4'-6'

Red Spot Croton — Shrimp Plant — Ti Red Sister — Lakeview Jasmine — Firespike

Ixora Super King — Plumbago — Podocarpus — Ruellia Purple Showers — Sanchezia

Variegated Arboricola — Pinwheel Jasmine — Viburnum — Zamia — Bleeding Heart

Snowbush — Curly Ruffle — Ixora Nora Grant — Thryallis — Silver Buttonwood

FULL SUN PLANTS

6'-8'

Cat Palm   Curly Ruffle   Roebelenii   Snowbush   Palmetto

Sanchezia   Caricature Plant   Ixora Nora Grant   Cocoplum   Starburst

Viburnum   Firebush   Podocarpus   Ixora Super King   Petrea

Jatropha   Confederate Jasmine   Variegated Arboricola   Silver Buttonwood   Lakeview Jasmine

Senna surattensis   White Bird   And. Crepe Hibiscus   Starburst   Roebelenii

8'-15'

Seminole Pink Hibiscus   Cattley Guava   Cocoplum   Silver Buttonwood   Podocarpus

Xmas Palm   Golden Senna   Jatropha   Lakeview Jasmine

15'-35'

Yellow Tab   Japanese Fern Tree   Geiger Tree   Cattley Guava   Macarthur Palm

15'-35'

Foxtail Palm   Travelers Palm   Thatch Palm   Silver Buttonwood   Sabal Palm

Fishtail Palm   Triangle Palm   Areca Palm   Chinese Fan Palm   Alexander Palm

Podocarpus   Bismarckia Palm

35'+

Royal Palm   Live Oak   Sabal Palm   Mahogany Tree   Queen Palm

Hong Kong Orchid   Coconut Palm   Gumbo Limbo   Pine Tree   Podocarpus

Laurel Oak   Royal Poinciana

Right: Ruellia Purple Showers, Cranberry Pentas, and Yellow Mussaendas make good companions for sun gardens.

Easy Sun Gardens

Before

After

Opposite top (Before): A sunny house in need of landscape renovation

Opposite bottom (After): A double Alexander Palm gives height in the center. Clumps of Ti Red Sisters form accents on each side. Pinwheel Jasmine surround the Red Sisters. Petra Crotons surround the palm. Jacob's Coat forms the border for the bed. This plant palette offers constant color with little care for many years, except for the Jacob's Coat, which lasts about six months, or however long it takes for the caterpillars to find it.

Above: The colors of the Corkscrew Crotons set the color scheme for this sunny bed. Notice the burgundy and yellow of the Crotons' leaves repeated in the yellow Allamandas and the burgundy Tis. This photo was taken in the summer, and the leaves of the Tis are dark. The photo on the opposite page was taken in winter, and the leaves of the same Ti Plants are bright pink.

CHAPTER 11

EASY GARDENS FOR SALT AND WIND

- ASSESSING SALT AND WIND

- PLANTS FOR MEDIUM OR HIGH SALT AND WIND

- PLANTS FOR HIGH SALT AND WIND

- GARDENS FOR SALT AND WIND

Above: This planting along the Intracoastal Waterway thrived with the moderate wind and salt it received. The combination includes Cranberry Pentas, Blue Daze, and Yellow Lantana. I have used this combination many times along this waterway with good success.

Left: Intracoastal site with medium salt and wind-tolerant plants: Cranberry Pentas and blue Plumbago. High winds burn these two plants.

Assessing Salt and Wind

Oceanfront Sites

Direct oceanfront sites (for example, on top of a dune) are easy to assess. They are very difficult for plants and need ones that can withstand high wind and salt. Areas very near the shoreline are traditionally landscaped with plants that are native to these areas. These plants are not within the focus of this book but are covered very well in "Seashore Plants of South Florida and the Caribbean" by David W. Nellis. Areas slightly back from the shore, but still within sight of the water, are ideal for the plants in this book that are classified as high salt and wind tolerant.

Sites along inland waterway or near the ocean but not directly on it

Plants with medium salt and wind tolerance do well in the majority of these sites. Exceptions include areas that are open to very wide expanses of water, where high winds are frequently a problem, or areas that get direct salt spray from a waterway. Use plants for high wind and salt in these locations. Other tricky locations are wind tunnels created by buildings. These frequently occur on the sides of buildings and definitely call for plants that are tolerant of high winds. Residents of these properties are the best sources of information about winds.

Expect wind damage on even the most tolerant plants

Every few years, Palm Beach County experiences a winter storm that brings 30 to 40 miles per hour winds to our beach areas for a few days in a row. About a month later, my phone starts to ring. Many people ask questions about why their landscape has so many brown tips on its leaves. Wind damage often shows up about a month after the wind event (unless, of course, it is a hurricane). It is mainly characterized by brown tips on the leaves. Even the most wind-tolerant plants, like Coconut Palms (which are native to beach areas all over the world), have brown tips on their leaves after a wind storm. The brown tips do not heal, but the leaves are eventually replaced with new growth. Occasionally tolerating brown leaf tips is a small price to pay for living near the ocean.

Hibiscus
Variegated Arboricola
Mammey Croton
Dwarf Crown of Thorns Rosy

A good plant palette for medium salt and wind: Hibiscus, Variegated Arboricola, Croton, Dwarf Crown of Thorns.

PLANTS FOR MEDIUM SALT AND WIND

Under 1'

Blue Daze — Mend Bromeliad — Purple Queen — Perfection Bromeliad — Juniper conferta

Liriope — Fire Croton — Foxtail Fern — Spider Lily — Ilex

1'-3'

Dwarf Ixora — Juniper Parsonii — Starburst Pentas — Crown of Thorns — Cranberry Pentas

Variegated Arboricola — Cocoplum — Lakeview Jasmine

Philodendron Xanadu — Plumbago — Podocarpus — Ruellia Purple Showers — Variegated Arboricola

2.5'-4'

Cocoplum — Silver Buttonwood — Dwarf Ixora — Shrub Allamanda — Cranberry Penta

Petra Croton — Ixora Super King — Red Spot Croton — Lakeview Jasmine — Jatropha

Snowbush — Ixora Nora Grant — Blue Porterflower

Plants for Medium Salt and Wind

4'-6'

Snowbush · Curly Ruffle · Plumbago · Ixora Nora Grant · Silver Buttonwood

Red Spot Croton · Ixora Super King · Lakeview Jasmine · Podocarpus · Ruellia Purple Showers

Zamia furfuracea · Shrub Allamanda · Cocoplum · Variegated Arboricola · Firebush

Jatropha · Petra Croton

6'-8'

Curly Ruffle · Roebelenii · Snowbush · Palmetto · Ixora Nora Grant

Cocoplum · Firebush · Podocarpus · Ixora Super King · Lakeview Jasmine

Variegated Arboricola · Confederate Jasmine · Jatropha · Silver Buttonwood

8'-15'

And.Crepe Hibiscus · Xmas Palm · Cattley Guava · Jatropha · Roebelenii

8'-15'
Seminole Pink Hibiscus | Silver Buttonwood | Lakeview Jasmine | Cocoplum | Podocarpus

15'-35'
Podocarpus | Chinese Fan Palm | Geiger Tree | Foxtail Palm | Sabal Palm

Thatch Palm | Silver Buttonwood | Alexander Palm | Bismarckia Palm

35'+
Live Oak | Gumbo Limbo | Royal Palm | Pine Tree | Sabal Palm

Podocarpus | Coconut Palm

Plants are frequently classified by either salt or wind tolerance. In gardens near the sea, both tolerances are important. The plants on this chart have at least medium tolerance of both salt and wind.

Right: Cast stone garden accessories like this fountain stand up well to salt and wind.

Plants for High Salt and Wind

Under 1'
Blue Daze   Purple Queen

1'-3'
Crown of Thorns   Ilex   Variegated Arboricola

2.5'-4'
Variegated Arboricola   Silver Buttonwood   Xanadu

4'-6'
Silver Buttonwood   Variegated Arboricola

6'-8'
Palmetto   Silver Buttonwood   Variegated Arboricola

8'-15'
Silver Buttonwood

15'-35'
Sabal Palm   Silver Buttonwood   Thatch Palm   Geiger Tree

35'+
Coconut Palm   Live Oak   Sabal Palm

Crown of Thorns, Crotons, and Purple Queens are good choices for salt and wind-tolerant color. Garden accessories, like this bird feeder, are also good choices for this a difficult environment.

EASY GARDENS FOR SALT AND WIND

Before

After

Above (Before): This site in Palm Beach is one block from the ocean. The home behind it created a wind tunnel effect for this garden. The plants in the pool area were severely wind damaged.

Right (After): Coconut Palms were planted in the hedge. The palms not only add to the tropical ambience of the pool but also act as a wind break for the most vulnerable side. The garden was very narrow, so a French lattice was placed in the center to give vertical impact. Variegated Arboricola are planted along the sides of the lattice. The accessories are made of cast stone, which is tolerant of all but hurricane force winds.

EASY GARDENS FOR SALT AND WIND

CHAPTER 12

EASY SMALL GARDENS

After

Before

Small gardens require more detail than large gardens because they are normally viewed from a short distance. Details show up that would be lost in a large street planting designed to be viewed at thirty miles per hour. Many Florida homes are wrapped around small gardens, with large windows overlooking the small space. The gardens become an extension of the home and are very important to the feeling of the house - inside as well as outside.

Above (Before): This garden was not only visually dull but also high maintenance. The hedges had to be trimmed once a month.

Left (After): High maintenance hedges were replaced with low maintenance color. The new garden requires trimming only two or three times a year. The Ti Red Sisters (plants with the bright pink to red leaves) provide dramatic color because they are planted in closely spaced clumps of many stems. Dwarf Crown of Thorns form the border, with Mammey Crotons in the middle.

Easy Small Gardens

Before

After

Left (Before): This planting area is only 16 inches wide. It is too narrow to fit enough layers to make an impact with plants. Since the house is built around this courtyard, this tiny planting bed is quite important. All major rooms of the house and guest house overlook it.

Below (After): Garden accessories provide the impact necessary to make an important design statement. French lattice marks the center. A glazed urn from tropical Asia completes the center focal point. Lattice obelisks break up the remaining space. Pink Angelwing Begonias and yellow Shrimp plants provide year-round color. Small planting beds surrounded by concrete are difficult environments for plants. They will not live as long as they would in a normal planting bed.

EASY SMALL GARDENS

Before

Above (Before): The Hibiscus in these planting beds are the wrong choice over pavement because they constantly drop leaves and flowers.

Right (After): Alexander Palms, Ti Red Sisters, Petra Crotons, and a border of Aztec Grass provide a neat and colorful solution.

After

EASY SMALL GARDENS

Before

Above (Before): Many people's initial response to seeing a blank wall like this one is "Cover it up!" The idea is not complete coverage, however, but to consider the wall an empty canvas. It needs an interesting landscape, with differences in height and texture.

Right (After): Queen Palms form the tallest layer, with Roebelenii Palms next highest. Ti Red Sisters, combined with Ti Sherberts, add tropical texture. Perfection Bromeliads and Liriope are planted as groundcover.

After

After

Before

- **EASY FLOWER GARDENS**

- **EASY MANICURED GARDENS**

- **EASY TROPICAL GARDENS**

- **EASY ECLECTIC GARDENS**

- **EASY NATURAL GARDENS**

Above (Before): This homeowner wanted to add old world charm to this house through landscaping.

Left (After): The home is transformed with a simple combination of plantings, a wall, and shutters. Queen Palms are arranged formally, while Confederate Jasmine climb the front wall and the chimney to add old world charm.

Easy Flower Gardens

Combine Cranberry Pentas, blue Plumbagos, and yellow Shrimp Plants for easy color. This garden is a favorite of butterflies. The Shrimps and Cranberry Pentas bloom all year, with the Plumbagos flowering most of the year.

Cranberry Pentas

Shrimp Plant

Plumbago

EASY FLOWER GARDENS

EASY FLOWER GARDENS

This combination is great for layering. Either the Yellow Mussaenda or the Ruellia Purple Showers works well as the back layer, with the other one in the middle. Cranberry Pentas form the border.

Ruellia Purple Showers

Yellow Mussaenda

Cranberry Pentas

Easy Manicured Gardens

Before

Left (Before): The best architectural feature of this home is the entry, which was obscured by the landscaping.

Right (After): The home looks completely different by simply uncovering its best feature, the entry, and accentuating it with plants. The look is manicured, which means the plants have a neat, sculpted quality. The spiral plants on either side of the front door are called topiaries, which are plants that have been trimmed into different shapes. They require monthly trimming. The low, dark green plant in front, the Sago Palm, is currently dying all over south Florida because of Cycad scale. Had I designed this garden today, I would have chosen a Cardboard Palm instead.

After

EASY MANICURED GARDENS

Before

After

Above (Before): A yard in need of renovation

Right (After): The homeowners decided on a manicured, minimalist look. The main design element is the pink marble gravel border, which defines the curves of the garden. The border is neatly contained with thin strips of black aluminum edging that hardly show but function well. The strips not only keep the two colors of gravels separate but also allow an edger to trim the grass without hitting the gravel. The bonsai bowls, planted with Mend and Perfection Bromeliads, form a center focal point.

After

After

EASY TROPICAL GARDENS

Before

Above (Before): As the trees in this garden grew, they produced too much shade for the shrubs and grass that were originally planted for full sun.

Right (After): The old plants were replaced with shade plants that give a tropical look. The key to a tropical look is a mix of textures, large-leaf tropicals with palms and small-leaf plants. The plants are layered, as they would appear in a natural forest. The large-leaf plant (with the banana-like leaves) is a White Bird of Paradise. The tallest palms are Queen Palms, of which only the trunks are visible in this photo. A Xmas Palm is near the center, with a Cat Palm at the end of the path. Petra Crotons and Ti Red Sisters add leaf color. Curly Ruffles are planted in front of the Crotons. Liriope and Bromeliads form the groundcovers.

After

EASY TROPICAL GARDENS

Bromeliads on trees are perfect for the low maintenance, tropical garden. To mount on trees, first soak some spaghnum moss in a bucket of water. Remove the plants from their pots and hold their root balls against the tree. Have a friend wring out handfuls of the moss like a sponge and hold them over the roots of the plants. Tie brown string (degradable) around the roots of the plants and the moss to secure the plants to the tree. Over time, some fall off and have to be re-tied. Be sure that the string will not cut into the tree as it grows. The goal is for the roots to train themselves to hold onto the tree without support. This is how most Bromeliads grow in nature.

Eclectic gardens are characterized by a mixture of different styles of plants. This garden mixes light textures, like Plumbago, which are thought of as cottage garden plants, with tropical textures, like Ti Plants and Sanchezias. The unifying factor is the curved bed line.

Coconut Palm

Ti Red Sister

Cranberry Pentas

Firespike

Snowbush

Plumbago

Yellow Mussaenda

Sanchezia

Ti Red Sister

EASY ECLECTIC GARDENS

Before

Left (Before): The medium shade in this garden does not provide enough light to support the St. Augustine grass.

Right (After): Medium shade plants replace the grass and transform the space. We do not have a shade groundcover that takes foot traffic in south Florida, so stepping stones and mulch provide a place to walk. These homeowners like a wide variety of plant material. The winding path unifies the mix. Starburst Pentas and Blue Daze line the screen enclosure and are mixed in with the more tropical looking plants to the left of the path. Alexander Palms are complemented by Ti Red Sisters and Petra Crotons.

After

EASY NATURAL GARDENS

The home pictured was built in a native Oak hammock, with the native trees, shrubs, and groundcovers saved rather than bulldozed. Some natives that work well in a natural setting are pictured on the right. From top to bottom: Firebush, Gumbo Limbo, and Geiger Tree.

Easy Natural Gardens

Before

Above (Before): A flagstone path winds through a native Pine and Sabal Palm forest.

Right (After): Shrubs and groundcovers were added to the path. A Mend Bromeliad shows well to the left of the path. Ti Red Sisters and Walking Iris appear on the right.

After

CHAPTER 14

EASY GARDEN PLANTING AND MAINTENANCE

KEYS TO EASY GARDEN PLANTING AND MAINTENANCE:

Prepare the soil easily and efficiently. Do not do a lot of unneeded work (page 306).

Plant in summer, if possible. Keep the root balls slightly out of the ground (pages 306-307).

Space the plants appropriately. The most common landscape mistake is over-planting (pages 308-311).

Trim infrequently but deeply. Many of the plants in this book only require trimming once or twice a year if they are properly placed (pages 312-317).

Use pre-emergent herbicides and contact herbicides as part of your weed control program. These products save a lot of time (page 316).

Fertilize with the right product in the right quantity at the proper time intervals. Done properly, it takes only 15 minutes three times a year to fertilize the shrubs, trees, and groundcovers in the average home (page 317).

Mulch once or twice a year with an organic product (page 318).

Control pests benignly, using toxic sprays as little as possible (page 319).

Water as little as possible once the plants are established (pages 224-237).

PLANTING

WHEN TO PLANT

Although planting is done all year in south Florida, summer is the best time to plant. Most people think that cooler weather offers better planting conditions than warmer weather. This is a common misconception, true only for winter annuals, like Impatiens. The plants in this book are acclimated for the subtropics and like the summer heat and rain. The goal is for the roots to grow immediately after planting. The heat and rain we receive in the summer cause the plant to grow faster, pushing the roots into the surrounding soil. Plants need water for establishment, and summer is when we have natural water. The only negative to summer planting is that, if we have a dry spell, you may have to water twice a day for a few days to keep the plants well hydrated. However, the likelihood of a dry spell in summer is low.

Winter is the most common planting time, however, probably because of lack of knowledge coupled with the fact that people are much more comfortable outside in our winters. Obviously, the plants do well when planted in winter. However, they establish and grow slower. Most people want their gardens to look their best in winter, when they spend most time outside and do the most entertaining. Gardens do not look filled in immediately after planting. They look their best after their first summer in the ground.

Another risk of winter planting is the likelihood of freeze damage. A freeze will damage plants that are recently planted more than those that are well established.

PREPARATION

Soils vary in south Florida, from sand to rock to marl. Check with your local county extension service about recommendations for preparing soil for planting in your immediate neighborhood. The plants in this book were tested in the sand of Palm Beach County with no soil preparation. When I first began designing, I recommended peat moss and compost. I specified that about one inch of each be tilled into the soil. At the end of two years, I compared the gardens with and without this soil preparation and saw no difference. A soil scientist told me that additives put on top of sand quickly wash through the soil. He recommended organic mulch because it is constantly breaking down and sending valuable organic matter into the soil, just like leaves in a natural forest. Organic mulch, with a slow-release fertilizer containing minor elements, applied three times a year, works as well as any soil preparation I have seen in good native sand.

Many new homes are built on fill soil that is very poor. The biggest problem I have run into is soil with a high percentage of shell that is compacted with steam rollers. This garden has the hardness of pavement, and the drainage is very poor. When you walk on the grass after a rain, you hear a squishing sound. Most plants do not do well in soil that does not drain. It is easy to tell neighborhoods with poor soil because many of the plants look sick. Contact local experts from your county extension service about how to handle these poor soils. Soil test labs are also very helpful. Look in the yellow pages and call a test lab for instructions on soil sampling if you are concerned about your soil.

With experience, you can look at the plants in an area and tell a lot about the quality of the soil. If the leaves are a good color of green and everything looks healthy, the soil is probably good.

If ordering soil to add to your beds, do not order top soil. It is too heavy. Order potting soil or 50% muck (or top soil) and 50% sand.

If you are creating new or large beds, you may need to remove sod. Healthy sod is very labor intensive to remove. Three steps are involved: cutting the sod roots so that it can be picked up, picking it up, and taking it away. Sod cutters are available from rental companies that cut the roots mechanically. They are heavy and difficult to use but an easier alternative than cutting it by hand. Sometimes, the sod comes up quite neatly and can be rolled up like a carpet and moved to another location. Other times, it comes up in little chunks that do not move well. Burying sod is an alternative to taking it away, but the rotting sod can cause a bad smell as it composts. Turn the page for more information on sod removal.

After removing the large pieces of sod, remove the small pieces and any other weeds or debris by hand. Then, rake the area smooth. If working near a building, be sure that the soil is higher near the building for drainage purposes.

Many people who move to south Florida from areas with clay soil cannot believe that the plants grow so well here, in most situations, with a minimum of soil preparation. Clay soil does not drain well, needing much work to prepare it to plant. In some ways, gardening is easier in Florida!

HOW TO PLANT

Planting is quite easy in areas of south Florida with sandy soil. It is difficult in areas with rocky soil or lots of tree roots. Landscape installation companies often use augers or mechanical digging tools to literally drill a hole in the rock to plant in rocky soils. Whatever the soil, follow these steps:

1. If the soil is difficult to dig in, either rent a mechanical digger or sharpen the edge of the shovel blade with an electric grinder. These grinders sell for about $30 at most hardware stores and are well worth it.
2. Dig a hole slightly wider and shallower than the root ball. Using a tape measure saves time.
3. Take the plant out of the pot. If any roots are circling, cut them slightly so they can grow straight into the soil and not in a circle.
4. Place the plant in the hole. Fill in the sides with the same soil. Do not put any additional soil on the top of the root ball. It should be slightly out of the ground, as shown in the diagram. The major cause of plant death after planting is planting too deep. Soil around the bottom of the plant rots the stem.
5. Water the plant so that the soil is well settled in the hole. Water thoroughly so that no air pockets remain around the root ball.

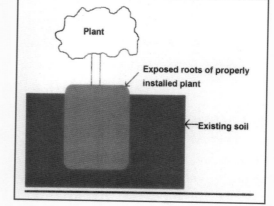

Plant

Exposed roots of properly installed plant

Existing soil

Planting a Back Yard

Step 1: Shrub removal

Using a sharp shovel (sharpen with an electric grinder, a useful and inexpensive tool found in any home center), cut a trench around the base of the shrub. Cut the roots that are uncovered with the shovel or a pair of clippers. Pull the shrub as far as possible in one direction. Cut the roots on the opposite side. Continue this root cutting until the shrub comes out of the ground.

Step 2: Mark Bed Lines

With a tape measure and a can of paint, mark the lines of the new bed. If you want to experiment a bit, use two colors of paint, white for your rough draft and a bright color for your final lines. If you make a mistake, the paint comes off in the next lawn cutting. Be sure the lines are clearly visible for the next step.

Step 3: Sod Cutting

Cutting the roots of the sod by hand so that it can be removed is very hard work. It is much easier to rent a sod cutter from your local rental company. Be sure you understand how the machine works, because they can be tricky. Follow the lines of the spray paint from Step 2.

STEP 4: SOD REMOVAL

Use a sharp shovel to cut the sod into pieces. Use a pitchfork to pick up the pieces and put them in a wheelbarrow. Shake off as much dirt as possible from the roots and leave it in the planting bed. Some hand removal of small pieces of sod is necessary. Rake the ground after removal to create a smooth, clean planting bed.

STEP 5: LAYOUT AND PLANT: LARGE PLANTS

Place the large plants first (in at least 7G or 14" diameter pots). Get them into a position that you like and plant them. Be sure to rotate each plant to put its best side forward! Plant according to the directions on page 307. Rake the soil after planting to make a smooth bed for the rest of the plants.

STEP 6: LAYOUT AND PLANT: SMALLER PLANTS

Place the smaller pots around the larger plants that are already in the ground. Get them into a position that you like and plant them. Plant each one at a slightly higher level than the existing soil. Rake the soil after planting to make a smooth bed for the fertilizer and mulch, but do not pile dirt up around any of the plants! Apply fertilizer. Spread mulch. Water thoroughly.

Planting a Front Yard

Step 1: Layout: Large Plants

Layout large plants first. If room allows, keep them about two feet away from the wall. The plants pictured are large Pink Angelwing Begonias in 15 gallon nursery pots. They are an excellent choice for height on the north side of a house. Notice how they are arranged in a triangular fashion. This staggering makes the layout look fuller and more natural. Follow the spacing guidelines for each individual plant species.

Step 2: Plant: Large Plants

Plant the large plants by digging a hole slightly larger than the root ball. Follow the planting instructions on page 307. After planting, rake the soil smooth to prepare a level bed for laying out the smaller plants.

Step 3: Layout: Back Row and Border

Layout the smaller plants that form the back row and the border. Ruellia Purple Showers form the back border, in between the Begonias. Cranberry Pentas form the border. Notice that the front edge of the border is at least 12 inches from the sod line, allowing room for future growth and edging.

STEP 4: STAGGER THE PLANTS

To form a mass, stagger the plant layout instead of placing them in a straight line. They fill in much better this way. Also, notice that these Ruellias are at least two feet from the wall of the house to give room for cleaning. Fewer insects enter a house if plants are not touching it.

STEP 5: LAYOUT: MIDDLE LAYER

Fill in the middle area. Shrimp Plants are evenly spaced between the Ruellias and the Cranberry Pentas.

STEP 6: PLANT SMALLER PLANTS, FERTILIZE, AND MULCH

Plant the smaller plants following the guidelines on page 307. Be sure to keep the root balls slightly out of the ground. Fertilize (page 317) and mulch (page 318). It takes three to six months for a planting like this to fill in so that the mulch is no longer visible.

LAYOUT AND PLANTING

LAYOUT TIPS

Layer plants with the tallest in the center of the grouping if it is viewed from all sides. Put the height in the back if it is viewed from one side only. The individual plant pages give layering ideas for each shrub and groundcover. Plan on a minimum of three layers. The garden to the right features Ti Red Sisters in the middle of a group of Alexander Palms. Shrub Allamanda is the shrub with the yellow flowers, bordered by Aztec Grass. The multicolored leaves in the background are the Corkscrew Croton.

Leave a mulch strip between the plants and the sod. This strip makes edging the grass easier, keeping the grass out of the planting beds. **Space plants appropriately.** Follow the guidelines on each plant page. Over-planting is common in south Florida and results in more disease, particularly fungus. Newly planted beds should not look filled in. The garden opposite features Corkscrew Crotons along the wall. Dwarf Powderpuffs have the red flowers in the foreground, with Shrub Allamanda under the palms. Aztec Grass forms the border.

Keep plants away from walls, if possible. This space is useful for cleaning the walls and helps in keeping ants out of the house. Sometimes it is not possible to keep plants away from walls because the planting space is just too small. If a bed is less than four feet wide, plant close to the wall. The same rule applies to hedges. The garden to the right features a triple Alexander Palm under-planted with Ti Red Sisters. Corkscrew Crotons line the wall. Purple Queen and Aztec Grass form the border.

Hand pruning is essential to maintain the appearance of most plants, especially flowering plants. The number one mistake made with flowering shrubs is to continually cut off the tips of the plants, which keeps them from flowering. Perennials need occasional deep cut-backs, as opposed to frequent tip-cutting. Each plant in this book has detailed trimming instructions on the individual plant pages. Many of the plants in this book only need occasional cut-backs. But, if they are not hand-pruned, they will be unacceptable landscape plants.

When to trim:
Each plant has its own optimal trim time, which is noted on the individual plant pages. Generally, trim immediately after flowering. For plants that bloom in the winter, trim in the summer. Trim summer bloomers as soon as they stop blooming in the fall. Plants recover from cut-backs faster in the summer months, so plants that bloom all the time, like Shrimp Plants, should be trimmed in the summer.

How much to trim:
Each plant has its own tolerances, so check the plant pages for specifics. Generally, most shrubs survive and thrive from hard cut-backs in the summer. It is possible to kill a plant from over-cutting, especially if all the leaves are removed. This is more likely in winter than summer.

Three steps to start:
1. Cut out any dead branches.
2. Remove any crossed branches that you can. Inspect the plant carefully. If you find crossed branches, visualize what the plant would look like without the least important of them. Remove it, if possible.
3. If two branches are growing parallel to each other, remove the weakest.

The structure of the plant is now defined. Proceed with trimming the rest of the plant. Avoid a boxy shape unless the plant is a square hedge. Think round. In natural plantings, curves are more pleasing to the eye than squares. Follow the shape of a dome when trimming, with the outside branches shorter than the middle, inside branches. Cut the branches at about a 45 degree angle.

Most plants send out two to three new shoots at each cut. This means you can double or triple the fullness of a shrub by trimming it.

Stagger-cutting versus hard cut-backs:
For many years, I recommended hard cut-backs on shrubs at least once a year. This process rejuvenates the plant but, also results in a month or two of looking at sticks. I still recommend this method for plants that bloom seasonally, like Firespike. It is easy to cut it way back after it stops blooming, and you do not miss any blooms because the plant does not bloom during that part of the year anyway. But, for plants that bloom all the time, like Shrimp Plants and Angelwing Begonias, I now stagger-cut, which keeps them full and blooming all the time. Simply cut the tallest branches to the ground two or three times a year, leaving the rest of the shrub intact. It is simple, fast, and very effective.

TRIMMING BY HAND

Tips for trimming Ti Plants:
Ti Plants are the worst maintained plants in south Florida. Since little is known about how to trim them, people ignore them until they look so bad they are finally removed. It takes about five minutes a year to trim your Ti Plants. The best time is March, when the leaves have some damage from the winter cold. Trim off any unsightly leaves and then stagger-cut and root the cuttings, as shown below:

Before

1. Trim off any brown or white leaves or leaf tips.
2. Trim off one third of the tallest branches to the ground.
3. Cut the branch that has been cut off into sections. Cut the top part of the branch off (the part with leaves) and stick it in the ground at the base of the plant.
Cut the wood part of the stem into sections at least 4" long. Stick them in the ground at the base of the plant, and they will root. (These photos were taken on the same day.)

After

Before

Renovation of Ti Plants in the landscape is easy to do. These pitiful Tis on the left are typical of most of the Tis in south Florida after they have been in the ground for a few years. The photo on the right shows the same Tis a few months after trimming them as shown above. Time of year is important. Trim in spring or early summer.

After

Before

After

Stagger-cutting Hibiscus: The shrub on the left had a good, basic structure. The purpose of the pruning was to maintain its good shape for the coming year. The parallel and crossed branches were removed. One third of the tallest branches were cut to the ground to encourage bottom branching. The remainder of the plant was cut like a dome, with the side branches shorter than the top.

Before

After

Stagger-cutting Allamanda: The same method used on the Hibiscus above was used on this Allamanda. Stagger cutting is very useful for most of the shrubs in this book because new growth is constantly appearing at the base, keeping the plant from getting leggy. Notice that the shrub is not squared off but cut in the shape of a dome.

Before

After

Hard cut-back on Jatropha: The Jatropha on the left was not a good candidate for stagger cutting because it did not have enough branches. The entire shrub was cut back very short. When done in the summer, most shrubs will develop three new branches for every branch cut, tripling the fullness of the shrub. Notice that leaves were left on the shrub. Removing all the leaves sometimes kills the shrub.

TRIMMING BY MACHINE AND WEEDING

Machine shearing is trimming the ends off of plants with electric or gas powered trimmers. This type of pruning is ideal for hedges or sculpted specimens because it is easier to square off a plant with a hedge trimmer than by hand. Certain plant materials (see photos below) are ideal for machine shearing because they grow dense, making good hedges. Trim hedges any time of year. Gas powered hedge trimmers are easier to use than electric because it is easy to cut the electric cord while trimming. The plants shown below are the only plants in this book that adapt well to machine shearing. Do not trim flowering material with hedge trimmers because you will cut off the flowers. Flowering plants that are continually machine-sheared stop blooming.

Lakeview Jasmine   Podocarpus   Viburnum   Ilex   Silver Buttonwood   Cocoplum

WEED CONTROL

Weeds are a maintenance challenge. They are so strong in south Florida that they even grow through the concrete on new expressways. How are they controlled with the least amount of time?

Weeds are the biggest problem right after planting. The soil has been disturbed, uncovering every weed seed in the area. Fertilizer has just been applied, which weeds like just as well as the other plants. And water is being applied heavily. The new plantings have lots of space in-between, which gives weeds room to grow. I suggest applying a pre-emergent herbicide on top of the mulch after the planting is completed. Pre-emergent herbicides do not hurt the existing plants. They simply inhibit weed seeds from germinating. Apply about every 90 days. These products inhibit about 70% of the weeds. There are many different types on the market. Follow the instructions closely.

What about the weeds that make it anyway? If they are a good distance away from the other plants, spray them with a contact herbicide. Contact herbicides are absorbed through the leaves of the plants, killing the roots underneath. Be very careful when using them, because they kill any leaves they come in contact with, including your new plantings, if you are not very careful. Spray in the early morning, when the wind is down. Herbicide drift (contact herbicide that hits plants you do not want to kill) is a common problem.

Weeds that sprout close to plants must be removed by hand. Mulch can cut down on them. Spacing your garden so that the plants will eventually grow together without leaving much light on the ground is another way to combat weeds.

Many weed cloths are on the market. Do not use plastic that will not absorb water because the water will not get to the roots of the plants. Do not use a weed cloth under mulch you want to break down to add organic material to the soil. If a weed cloth is placed under paths or other areas that are not planted, the mulch or gravel must be thick enough to cover it very well.

Fertilization used to be quite difficult in south Florida. The products were tricky to use, with complicated instructions regarding tilling in the fertilizer, watering in the mix, etc. We killed our first lawn by applying just a little too much. Another complication was buying many different products in order to give the plants all the nutrients they needed to thrive. Times have changed. Many of the newer, slow-release mixes are very easy to use and include all the elements the plants need to live.

Plants need 16 elements to grow. Most people are familiar with the major three elements: nitrogen (N), phosphorus (P), and potassium (K). The large numbers (like 13-13-13, for example) on the fertilizer bags indicate the proportion of each of these elements in the mix.

The other 13 elements also play critical roles in the health of south Florida plants. We call these minor elements or minors, and our soils are devoid of many of them. The less expensive fertilizers include few minors, and you can waste a lot of effort applying them, only to find your plants do not respond well to them. Look for a mix that includes magnesium, boron, copper, iron, manganese, and molybdenum. The ingredients are listed on the fertilizer package. If the mix does not include minor elements, do not buy it. Even some expensive, slow-release fertilizers do not include these crucial elements.

Fertilizers are applied in either a granular, dry form or as a liquid. Liquid fertilizers (usually a blue powder that is mixed with water in a hose-end sprayer) show results faster, but only last a few weeks. Granular fertilizers are the norm because they generally last for three months. The average yard needs three types: one for the lawn, one for the shrubs, groundcovers, and shade trees, and one for the palms, if they are present. Slow-release mixes are the best because they last longer and are released slowly.

Fertilize three times a year: March, June, and October. If leaves on your plants turn yellow, fertilize again. This happens most often in the summer, when we have very heavy rains.

Carefully follow the instructions on the fertilizer package when you first begin using a product. Do not guess. Using too much may kill plants, and not enough is a wasted effort. Plants need careful fertilizations for at least their first year in the ground. After plants are well-established, I still fertilize three times per year, but I do not use as much as I used the first year. Many of the plants in this book are well adapted to our native soils and need less supplemental feeding as the years progress. Keep a heavy layer of mulch on your planting beds. The mulch is continuously breaking down into many of the elements that are in a fertilizer bag.

If you are in a new community and have a lot of shell in the soil, you may have to fertilize more frequently than in neighborhoods with better soil. Watch your plants, and they will show you what they need. Well fed plants have green leaves and look healthy.

Applying fertilizer to shrubs and groundcovers is very easy, if you purchase the right product. I can do most yards in about 10 or 15 minutes. Fertilizing a lawn takes longer and requires a spreader, but it is still easy. Palms are more difficult because they require large quantities of heavy fertilizer. Also, palm fertilizers can burn surrounding shrubs. You may want to hire a professional to take care of palm fertilization.

MULCHING

When I first began gardening in south Florida, I had a hard time keeping my plants healthy. After many years of research, I learned the importance of fertilizers with minor elements, judicious watering, and organic mulches. Mulches are critical for the low maintenance garden. Plan on mulching your garden once or twice a year. Twice a year is ideal. Organic mulch conserves water, inhibits weeds, adds organic matter to the soil, and improves the look of the garden. South Florida soils are not attractive, and mulch covers them up.

Types of organic mulches vary. Cypress is the most common. It comes in three grades: B minus, B plus, or Grade A. B minus is ground-up wood, B plus is a combination of ground wood and bark, and Grade A is all ground bark. Ground bark is preferable to ground-up wood because it keeps its color longer and does not float. Although Grade A mulch is more expensive, it lasts much longer and does not float away with the next rainstorm.

Eucalyptus mulch is attractive and lasts a long time. However, it does not cover as much ground as Cypress mulch, making it much more costly.

Pine straw is wonderful mulch because it keeps its dark brown color, is very attractive, and acidifies the soil. It is quite expensive, however. I often use Pine straw on paths, where it shows, and less expensive Cypress mulch in the planting beds.

Pine bark is not recommended in large sizes because Palmetto bugs (giant roaches) nest in it. The Pine bark mini-nuggets are a great mulch.

Many tree trimming companies and power companies offer free mulch. The quality of this mulch varies widely, depending on the type of trees and the type of machine used to grind the mulch. Usually, it is available by the truckload only, which is normally ten cubic yards. Ten cubic yards covers an area of 1600 square feet to a depth of two inches. Some tree companies will let people come to their offices, look at their mulch, and take away a smaller amount than a truckload.

When comparing mulch prices, look at the quantity per bag. Bag sizes vary from one cubic foot to three cubic feet. With Cypress mulch, B plus mulch normally comes in bags that are two cubic feet and covers 12 square feet of ground. Grade A mulch is usually in bags that contain three cubic feet, which covers 20 square feet of ground.

Apply mulch to a depth of two inches wherever possible. Do not put it up against the trunk of a tree or a small plant. Mulch can rot or smother a small plant. Annuals are often left without mulch or with a band of mulch edging the bed but not up against the little plants.

South Florida soils are low in organic matter. Plants need organic matter to thrive. Organic mulches provide a constant breakdown of organic matter, like leaves in a natural forest.

The plants in this book do not attract many pests, so do not make the common mistake of using toxic chemicals to prevent bugs from arriving. Many garden sprays commonly sold are very poisonous and should never be used unless absolutely necessary. Some sprays are capable of killing birds, butterflies, dogs, cats, and humans, so take great care with pesticides.

My test gardens have been sprayed once in five years. We sprayed with a fungicide after a tropical storm dropped 18 inches of rain in 24 hours, and the garden was underwater for three days. If I see holes in the leaves, I watch them for a few days or weeks. If the plants are healthy, the bugs usually stop eating. Keep your plants well fertilized, mulched, and wisely watered, and you will not see many pests in your garden. My garden is in a natural woods, which makes it easier for me to control pests because I have good predators to eat bad pests in the garden.

Suburban houses are sometimes more of a problem, particularly if anyone nearby is spraying heavily. Spraying kills the good bugs as well as the bad, and toxic chemicals disrupt natural controls.

Plants are particularly vulnerable to pests immediately after planting. They are in a weakened state and actually send out signals that attract pests. Watch your plants closely for three to six months after planting. If you see bugs on the plants, they are normally very easy to remove. Aphids, for example, are clustered on the ends of branches, eating the new growth. They look like little dots. Simply remove them by cutting the tip off the plant and throwing it away. If they return, spray the plant with something that makes it taste bad to them. They do not like soap, garlic, or pepper, and none of these will kill birds, butterflies, or people. Garden centers sell sprays with these natural products as their base.

If you see holes in the leaves of a plant and cannot find the bugs, they are probably snails or caterpillars. Snails have been the single biggest pest problem I have seen in south Florida. Most snails and caterpillars stay hidden in the daytime, feeding only at night. If the damage becomes severe, you need to do something, or you could lose the plants. Snail bait is commonly sold in garden centers. Follow the instructions closely. Most brands are easy to apply. The majority of people do not follow the instructions closely, applying the bait only once when the box says to apply it more times. The snails will return if the bait is not properly applied. A natural method of snail control is also available. Fill a low bowl with beer. Bury the bowl in the garden so the rim is level with the surface of the soil. The snails, attracted to the beer, will fall in the bowl and drown happily.

For caterpillars, ask your garden center which product they recommend that will take care of caterpillars without harming birds, cats, dogs, or people.

Fungus is another problem in south Florida. Fungus thrives in wet areas. On the plant pages, I have recommended trimming plants that have a susceptibility to fungus during the rainy periods. If fungus becomes severe, ask your garden center for the least toxic alternative and follow the instructions closely.

BIBLIOGRAPHY

Baensch, Ulrich, Ph.D. and Ursula. Blooming Bromeliads. Nassau/Bahamas: Tropic Beauty Publishers, 1994.

Bar-Zvi, David. Tropical Gardening. New York: Pantheon Books, Knopf Publishing Group, 1996.

Broschat, Timothy K. and Meerow, Alan W. Betrock's Reference Guide to Florida Landscape Plants. Holly wood, Florida: Betrock Information Systems, 1999

Brown, B. Frank ED.D. Crotons of the World. Valkaria, Florida: Valkaria Tropical Garden, 1992.

Brown, B. Frank ED.D. The Cordyline, King of Tropical Foliage. Valkaria, Florida: Valkaria Tropical Garden, 1994.

Crawford, Pamela and Helms, Kathy. "The New Florida Landscape". Unpublished masters thesis, 1990.

Haele, Robert G., and Brookwell, Joan. Native Florida Plants. Houston, Texas: Gulf Publishing Company, 1999.

Holttum, R.E. and Enoch, Ivan. Gardening in the Tropics. Singapore: Times Editions, 1991.

MacCubbin, Tom, and Tasker, Georgia. Florida Gardener's Guide. Franklin, Tennessee: Cool Springs Press Inc., 1997.

Meerow, Alan W. Betrock's Guide to Landscape Palms. Hollywood, Florida: Betrock Information Systems. 1999.

Menninger, Edwin A. Flowering Trees of the World. New York: Hearthside Press Inc. 1962.

Nellis, David W. Seashore Plants of South Florida and the Caribbean. Sarasota, Florida: Pineapple Press. 1994.

Stresau, Frederic B. Florida My Eden. Port Salerno, Florida: Florida Classics Library, 1986.

Watkins, John V. and Sheehan, Thomas J. Florida Landscape Plants. Gainesville, Florida: University Presses, 1975.

Bold page numbers indicate main
plant information pages.

*Italicized page numbers indicate
addtional photos.*

Bold page numbers indicate main plant information pages.

Italicized page numbers indicate addtional photos.

Learn the secrets to a revolutionary, new container system in Pamela Crawford's new book, *Instant Container Gardens* (available May, 2007).

Planting is As Easy as One, Two, Three!

Step 1: Add soil up to the first hole. Wet the root balls of the plants and squeeze them. Slide the root balls through the holes.

Step 2: Plant the centerpiece.

Step 3: Plant the edge plants.

Before - 16" wall pot

One week later!